GHOSTS AND LEGENDS OF NORTHERN OHIO

WILLIAM G. KREJCI

Haunted America

Published by Haunted America
A Division of The History Press
Charleston, SC
www.historypress.net

First published 2019

Manufactured in the United States

ISBN 9781467141444

Library of Congress Control Number: 2019943354

CONTENTS

Contents

CONTENTS

ACKNOWLEDGEMENTS

I would like to thank the following for their priceless contributions to this work. First and foremost, special thanks go to Ryan McCarbery, who joined me on almost every road trip and kicked around some wonderful ideas. It's a safe bet that this book wouldn't exist without his assistance.

I would also like to thank John Rodrigue, Ben Gibson, Sara Miller and the staff at The History Press; Randy Bergdorf; the Peninsula Library and Historical Society; Alison Lawson; Arrye Rosser; the National Park Service; Cuyahoga Valley National Park; Thomas A. Krejci; George and Mary Krejci; Jennifer Dobbins; Craig Whitmore; Christina Johnson; Jackie Smith; Matthew Rump; Chestnut Grove Cemetery; the City of Olmsted Falls; Charles Cassady Jr.; John Lewis; West Branch State Park; the Ohio Department of Natural Resources; Cassie Maiorana; Krista Horrocks; David Wright; Rich Tarrant; the Vermilion History Museum; Geoff Hanks; Julie Hanks; Sean Lavelle; Amy Mazzocco; Kim Anderson; James A. Willis; Gavin Esposito; Maren McKee; Tom Finnerty; Terry Lipply; the Ashtabula Public Library; Callyn Cooley; the Seneca County Museum; the Oberlin Heritage Center; the Cuyahoga Falls Historical Society; the Cleveland Public Library; Shane and Amy Moore; the Williams family; Wolf Creek Tavern; Susan Ebert and Westside Steve Simmons; the Lake County Recorder's Office; the Summit County Recorder's Office; the Richfield Historical Society; Darcy Miller and the Old Stone House Bed and Breakfast; Elaine Crane and the Rider's Inn; Carl Thomas Engel; the Morley Library; the Sandusky Library; the Library of Congress; Valerie Renner; the Akron Civic Theatre; the *Akron Beacon Journal* and Ohio.com; Ray Hall; Ellen Herman; Tom Miller; and the Sandy and Beaver Canal Association.

INTRODUCTION

I was fourteen years old when I first heard the legend of Gore Orphanage. It was a fall afternoon in 1989, and a group of us were skateboarding in front of our friend Geoff's house when the subject of ghost stories came up. Another friend was telling us about a grave site that was said to be haunted by the ghost of the executed witch who was buried there. At this, Geoff related the story of Gore Orphanage, the haunted ruins of a children's home in western Lorain County that met its end at the hands of a mad caretaker. When Geoff's mother returned home an hour later, she filled in the parts of the story that he couldn't remember.

That was it. I was hooked.

Up until that point, the only ghost story that intrigued me was that of the Franklin Castle in Cleveland. Discovering this new legend in my home county was exciting, to say the least.

Two more years passed before I saw Gore Orphanage Road in person. By that time, a slightly different tale surrounding the circumstances of the orphanage's downfall was being told. It was hard to know what to believe. More than anything else, I just wanted to know the truth. Literature on the subject was greatly limited. Still, I decided that I would make every effort to uncover the true story behind this Northern Ohio legend.

Along the way, other tales of local hauntings were passed along to me. More and more, I was hearing stories of witches' graves and crybaby bridges. It seemed like every county had one. I wondered if there was a shred of truth to any of it. My career as an investigative historian was born out of this.

The unfortunate thing is that sometimes you end up bursting people's bubbles. After all, truth is the goal, not perpetuating and regurgitating the falsehoods that have been passed along for years. By shedding light on these stories, we sometimes kill our favorite legends. I'm quite sure that I won't make many friends by writing this book.

I should state at the onset that I'm not out to debunk any hauntings. Besides, that's impossible. With the exception of someone coming forward and admitting that they made the whole thing up, I can no more debunk a haunting than I can prove it. I can tell you that a place is haunted until I'm blue in the face, but that doesn't necessarily make it so. It's not proof.

That's not the purpose of this book, anyway. What I intend to do is share these ghostly legends and reveal their true backstories. Along the way, we may even stumble upon the origins of the legends. These tend to be hidden in newspaper articles published around the time of the events that play into the original stories. Some mysteries will be solved, and a few forgotten mysteries will be rediscovered. This book won't disappoint in either of these regards.

Also, just as it's impossible to prove or disprove a haunting, the same can be said of identifying or putting a name to a ghost that haunts a location. Of course, guesses can be made. We tend to base these on people who met tragic ends at these sites, but again, it doesn't make it so.

Some of the stories that follow will be familiar. Some will be, well, not-so-familiar. What you won't see are stories of Ohio Sasquatch, alien encounters or tales of Melon Heads. I'm not a cryptozoologist. Alien encounters aren't ghostly urban legends. The idea of a woodland-dwelling colony of hydrocephalic cannibal dwarfs living near Kirtland is preposterous, despite what your uncle's friend says he saw out there in 1986. You get the picture.

CHAPTER I

HELLTOWN

A Legend Retold

Whenever the topic of Northern Ohio ghostly legends is brought up, it isn't long before someone starts talking about a place called "Helltown." There are a multitude of stories attached to that location, thus it seems like a great starting point for this book.

Nestled in the winding Cuyahoga Valley sits an abandoned town that has become the subject of ghostly legends and government conspiracies. Rumors tell of a toxic waste spill that spurred the government to force mass evacuations. The disaster, it's said, was covered up with the development of a national park. Further tales speak of an abandoned school bus where children are said to have been viciously murdered. A Satanic cult is said to hide behind the guise of a Catholic church. A haunted house sits alone and deserted in the woods, yet a light is always seen at night. Stories are told of a spectral hearse that prowls an abandoned road, gathering souls to usher into hell, and an old slaughterhouse near the graveyard is suspected as a hotbed of ghostly activity. Not surprisingly, Helltown is also said to harbor a crybaby bridge and at least two haunted cemeteries.

One of the signs placed on the boarded-up homes in the Cuyahoga Valley. *Photo by William G. Krejci.*

In 2017, a film called *Helltown*, which billed itself as a documentary, was released. A closer look reveals that the entire production was fabricated. The first clue that it's a fake should be that a man who claims to be a professor of folklore and mythology at Cuyahoga Community College doesn't even know how to pronounce the word "Cuyahoga." The story centers around the idea that a mythical creature called a wendigo stalks the area, while most of the core legends are avoided. Since the ideas presented in the so-called documentary are ridiculous and have been debunked by many other investigators, the topic will not be covered here.

ORIGIN OF THE STORY AND NAME

The legend of Helltown is primarily centered around Boston Township in Summit County. Specifically, the story is concentrated on the town of Peninsula and a former village called Boston. Some stories extend beyond these locations and spill over into neighboring Boston Heights and Brecksville.

The true tale begins around 1974, when the federal government passed legislation that created the Cuyahoga Valley National Recreation Area. This came on the heels of the Clean Water Act of 1972. The Cuyahoga River made worldwide headlines when it caught fire in 1969. Converting the river valley south of Cleveland into a protected site seemed like a natural course of action.

A controversy arose when the government, through eminent domain, seized a number of residential properties and farms that were originally to remain in private hands. At first, it was said that people living within the boundaries of the new National Recreation Area could remain in their homes, but soon after, the National Park Service deemed these homes to be obstructions to the natural beauty of the area. After the takeover, which sparked outrage and protests, many of the houses sat empty, while others were burned down to provide training for firefighters. The vacant houses bore government signs that warned against trespassing. Anyone driving through the area who saw this would naturally become suspicious. A documentary called *For All People, For All Time* details the controversy surrounding the land seizures.

In 2000, the Cuyahoga Valley National Recreation Area was redesignated as Cuyahoga Valley National Park and now contains over thirty-two thousand acres.

One of many boarded-up houses in Boston Township during the 1970s. The Krejci house, pictured here, was ultimately demolished. *Courtesy Peninsula Library & Historical Society.*

Randy Berrgdorf, director of the Peninsula Historical Society, suggests that the name Helltown began as "Hale Town." This refers to the nearby Hale Farm and Village, a re-created pioneer settlement operated by the Western Reserve Historical Society that sits southwest of Peninsula. People may have been referring to Peninsula as Hale Town, as it's the closest actual town to that attraction.

Interestingly, there was a place previously known as Hell Town in Ohio. Located just south of Pleasant Hill Lake in Richland County, it was a Lenape Indian settlement that existed from the 1770s until 1782. Originally called Clear Town, it was named for nearby Clear Creek but was referred to as Hell Town by Moravian missionaries (the word "hell" is the German word for bright or clear).

As far as the name Helltown being associated with Boston Township is concerned, references to this in newspapers or books don't predate the late 1990s.

Crybaby Bridge

It's said that the bridge spanning the Cuyahoga River at Boston Mills Road was once the site of a horrific case of infanticide. The story claims that in the 1800s, a woman threw her unwanted child over the side of the bridge, casting it to its death in the dark river below. Visitors to the site at night claim to hear the sounds of the child's cries and witness the ghostly apparition of the mother, who's said to be dressed in white. As with many such haunted crossings, the Helltown crybaby bridge involves a ritual for summoning the ghosts.

Anyone who visits the site today will be surprised to discover that a bridge of such ghostly legend can appear so inviting. The fact is that it's a relatively newer bridge. Even at that, the bridge it replaced wasn't the original structure. Does a ghost continue to haunt a bridge even if it's not the original one?

Interestingly, the Boston Mills Road bridge that existed when the story is said to have taken place was a covered bridge. Its sides were enclosed, which would've made it quite impossible to throw a baby over the side. It appears that this fact was overlooked when the story was concocted.

Old covered bridge at Boston, circa 1890. View is looking southeast across the river. *Courtesy Cuyahoga Valley National Park.*

THE ROAD TO HELL

Legends abound of a road at Helltown that's been closed to the public. Some stories refer to it as the Road to Hell, the Highway to Hell, the Road to Nowhere or even as the Road to the End of the World. Located along this road were many abandoned houses that have since vanished. Some claim that drivers on this road find themselves overwhelmed by an urge to drive off into the deep Brandywine Gorge to the north. Others say that the road is haunted by the ghosts of those who've gone to their deaths in the countless auto accidents on the road. People have claimed to witness a ghostly hearse driving along the road at night.

The site of this legend is Stanford Road, which once connected the village of Boston with a small community that existed at Brandywine Falls. After the federal government seized area properties in the 1970s, nearly every house on Stanford Road sat empty. Eventually, they were torn down. Since there were no longer any residents on Stanford Road, Boston Township decided to cease road maintenance. Over the years, the road has started to crumble into Brandywine Creek, so it's been closed to traffic and is now a hiking trail.

One area resident did own a hearse but has since sold it. There have never been any fatal auto accidents on Stanford Road.

THE HOUSE IN THE WOODS

Another legend of Helltown claims that an abandoned haunted house sits in the woods and that a mysterious light emanates from it. The house this tale refers to is the Stanford House, which is located near the spot

The Stanford House, which now serves as a hostel. *Photo by William G. Krejci.*

15

where Stanford Road is closed. The Greek Revival home was built around 1843 by George Stanford. It was purchased by the government in 1978 and added to the Cuyahoga Valley National Recreation Area. On June 7, 1986, it reopened as a hostel, thus a light is regularly seen coming from the building. It should be noted that this house is not abandoned, as it continues to operate as a hostel, nor is it located in the woods. No historic record exists of it being haunted.

THE MURDER BUS

Located in the woods near Helltown is a bus that's rumored to have been the scene of a grisly murder. The most common tale says that the bus was hijacked by an escaped mental patient while it was dropping off children from school one afternoon. The story says that he drove the bus to a nearby wooded area and massacred the children, whose otherworldly cries of terror reverberate through the empty vehicle to this day.

In truth, there never was such an incident, and the whole story was created to simply add to the ghostly area legends. Shortly before the government purchased the properties in the area, a house was being renovated, and the owner brought in an old school bus to live in while the renovations took place. When the property was taken over by the government, the bus was left behind. Following complaints from neighbors, the National Park Service had it removed.

CULTISTS' CHURCH

One of the stories that was covered in the "documentary" about Helltown was the tale of a Satanic cult operating out of a church. The church in question is actually Mother of Sorrows Church in Peninsula. According to the Catholic Diocese of Cleveland, the congregation was established in 1882.

The Satanic cult stories were traced to architectural details that can be found on the front of the church—two sets of crossbeams that seem to form upside-down crosses. People overlook the fact that an upright cross is plainly mounted on the top of the bell tower. The idea that a Satanic cult operates out of this location is preposterous.

Mother of Sorrows Church in Peninsula. *Photo by William G. Krejci.*

HAUNTED CEMETERIES

It's been claimed that Helltown is home to at least two separate haunted cemeteries. One of these is Mater Dolorosa Cemetery, which is located in the woods just east of the Happy Days Lodge and is associated with Mother of Sorrows Church. Originally, this was part of the Cassidy farm. It's a beautiful little burial ground with no organized layout and a small footpath winding down the middle. Of interest is the grave of Private Thomas C. Coady, a Civil War soldier and former prisoner of war who was killed on April 27, 1865, when the steamship *Sultana* exploded on the Mississippi River, taking 1,169 souls with it. His remains were recovered and buried three days later.

Boston Cemetery, 1970s.
*Courtesy Cuyahoga Valley
National Park.*

The other cemetery that figures into the story is Boston Cemetery, which is located at the north end of Main Street in Boston. It's believed that this hilltop burial ground was originally a Native American earthwork. This should be of little surprise. There are numerous such mounds located in the Cuyahoga Valley. Of note is the burial site of John Brown, a well-known counterfeiter. Sadly, Boston Cemetery has experienced vandalism since the emergence of the Helltown legend.

Both sites claim to host ghostly apparitions, but visitors to either cemetery should take caution. Cemeteries are only open during daylight hours. Visiting after sunset, as well conducting paranormal research or investigations of any kind at either site, will result in legal action. A sign at the entrance of Boston Cemetery clearly states: "Activities other than meditation and reverence for those remembered here shall be prosecuted to the fullest extent of the law."

THE SLAUGHTERHOUSE

Near Boston Cemetery sits an old building said to once have served as a slaughterhouse. Other tales say that it was used as a funeral home. Original stories claimed that the old building was haunted by ghostly faces that appeared in the windows. Later versions slightly confused the legend to say that faces appeared when someone looked inside through a window. Of course, there's no way to substantiate either of these claims.

The truth about the building is that it never served as a slaughterhouse or funeral home. It was an outbuilding that was used as employee housing, nothing more. It sits entirely on private property. Looking in the windows doesn't bring ghostly appearances—it brings police officers.

THE TOXIC WASTE DUMP

The original legend of Helltown claims that the entire area was the scene of a toxic chemical spill and that the evacuation of the area was covered up with a story that the region was being turned into a national park. Believe it or not, this legend has some basis in fact.

In 1940, John Krejci II converted his 200-acre farm, located east of Boston on Hines Hill Road, into a dump. This property was split by the construction of Interstate 271 in 1972, leaving 179 acres. In 1980, 42.5 acres of the dump were acquired by the government to be included in the Cuyahoga Valley National Recreation Area. The Krejci family received $516,000 for the land.

The dump continued to operate through 1985. A year later, park rangers visiting the area complained of headaches, nausea and rashes. The EPA took soil samples and found that they were contaminated with hazardous materials, including arsenic, heavy metals, polyaromatic hydrocarbons and other potential cancer-causing agents. Initial cleanup estimates were $6 million. Final costs ran as high as $50 million. The Krejci Dump was designated a Superfund cleanup site. Remediation of the land was completed around 2012.

Entrance to the Krejci Dump, circa 1981. *Courtesy Cuyahoga Valley National Park.*

It should be noted that when John Krejci II began accepting materials, they weren't designated as hazardous. He was repurposing much of what was dumped and wasn't charging for disposal. Also, the government claimed not to know about the site being used as a toxic waste dump. In truth, the government was made aware of the situation when Interstate 271 was built, but that information wasn't passed along to the National Park Service.

The Helltown legend states that the evacuations around Boston Township came on the heels of a toxic waste spill. The presence of toxic materials at the Krejci Dump was not kept secret, nor was it covered up. Furthermore, its presence wasn't realized by the National Park Service until twelve years after the properties were taken over by the government.

One final note: The author of this book is not related to the Krejci family that operated this facility. Please stop asking.

A Legend Concluded

The place that legend hunters call "Helltown" is truly a beautiful and picturesque location, and a visit to the area is highly recommended, but for the right reasons. Cuyahoga Valley National Park features a recreational hike and bike trail that follows the old towpath for the Ohio and Erie Canal. At the village of Boston sits the old Boston Store and the park's Boston Mill Visitor Center. The Cuyahoga Valley Scenic Railroad meanders along the rails of the old Valley Railway, and excursions are always a great way to enjoy a leisurely afternoon. Nearby Virginia Kendall Ledges are a geological feature worth exploring.

The villages of Boston and Peninsula, neither of which are abandoned or ghost towns, feature many wonderful shops and restaurants. Both contain natural and historic points of interest that should also be visited. On a snowy day, the Village of Peninsula resembles an image from a Christmas card.

As far as Helltown is concerned, the people who live in the area are sick of the story. Ordinances are in place to prevent ghost-hunting at many of the sites described in the legends. Also, most of these locations are on private property, and trespassing is an offense punishable to the fullest extent of the law.

In conclusion, don't go looking for Helltown. Asking area residents for directions to Helltown is equally inadvisable—since they won't be able to give you directions to a place that doesn't exist and never has, they may be able to tell you where else you can go.

CHAPTER II

WITCHES' GRAVES

INTRODUCTION

A dark cemetery at midnight. Autumn leaves rustling at your feet. An ancient tree with a mysteriously low branch. A depression in the ground where a burial must be located. These are the images that may come to mind when one thinks of the old witches' graves that we've heard so much about since we were young. The truth may surprise you.

THE WEST BRANCH WITCH

One of the best examples showing the evolution of a witch's grave legend comes from West Branch Sate Park in Portage County, where the woods are said to be haunted by a ghostly witch who appears in the form of a woman in black. Things didn't start out that way.

The story begins around 1960, when B.A. Evans, who'd recently purchased a property in Edinburg Township, made the discovery of a small cemetery hidden in the woods on his land. It was a curious-looking burial ground that contained seven gravestones and was surrounded by a sandstone wall forty inches high. Evans cleared it of the weeds and brush that had been choking it out for years. The graves contained in the little cemetery belonged to the Elliott family, who had settled the area during the first half of the nineteenth century.

Mulford B. Elliott was born in New York in 1801. He traveled to Portage County, where he met Elizabeth "Betsey" Bowles of Pennsylvania. The two married in 1826 and settled in the village of East Davis in Edinburg Township, Portage County. They became the parents of ten children, five of whom were buried in the family cemetery.

The first of these was Mulford and Betsey's five-month-old daughter, Melissa, who died on May 7, 1837. Her headstone was missing when the cemetery was rediscovered by Evans. The second burial was Melissa's eight-year-old brother, Mulford Elliott Jr., who died on January 5, 1841. Three months later, another child, Wesley, died at only one and a half days old. April 23, 1854, saw the death and burial of Mulford and Betsey's ten-month-old grandson, John Elliott Jewell. Louisa Jewell, John's mother, was the last person buried there, with her death occurring on August 25, 1892.

Betsey Bowles Elliott passed away on January 28, 1870, and was laid to rest with her family in the little cemetery. Mulford B. Elliott died on June 17, 1878, in Angola, Indiana. His son Samuel, who then owned the family farm, had his father's remains returned to Ohio for burial. Samuel Elliott erected the stone wall that surrounds the cemetery.

There was one more burial at that location—a daughter of Mulford and Betsey who died in 1864. Her headstone read:

CLAMENZA ISADORE
Dau. of
M.B. & B. ELLIOTT
BORN
July 8, 1847
DIED
Dec. 27, 1864
AGED
17 yrs 4 ms 19 ds.
Remember youth as you pass by.
As you are now, so once was I.
As I am now, so must you be.
Prepare for death and follow me.

Shortly after Evans made his discovery, stories began to circulate about the odd little cemetery and the curious inscription on Clamenza Elliott's

The ruins of the Elliott family cemetery in Portage County. *Photo by William G. Krejci.*

headstone. Wiser people recalled this being an old-fashioned epitaph that was used for centuries. More gullible individuals took it to be a warning—or worse yet, a hex. Thus, a legend of a witch's grave was born.

An alternative origin comes from a woman named Mrs. Sampson who grew up in a stone house in the area. The house, which no longer exists, was located in the valley below the cemetery and was taken when the West Branch of the Mahoning River was dammed. Mrs. Sampson claimed that she used to sled down the hill near the Elliott family cemetery when she was a child and that she and her friends started the story about the witch. They were quite young at the time and were frightened by the old cemetery. The fact that Clamenza Elliott was so young when she died and had such a strange inscription on her tombstone had them believing that she was a witch.

The generally accepted legend claims that Clamenza was killed by locals for her practices in the dark arts and was buried on her family's farm. She'd appear at night in the form of a woman dressed in black and chase away anyone who disturbed her resting place.

Someone who recalls these legends as dating back as far as the early 1960s is David Wright, who was a volunteer at West Branch State Park for seven years. Wright used to go camping at Camp Carl and often heard the stories of the witch who haunted the woods in the area.

Shortly after David Wright started camping in the area, the Michael J. Kerwin Dam was erected on the West Branch of the Mahoning River. In 1966, the land surrounding the reservoir became West Branch State Park. The old Elliott farm and cemetery sat along what had once been West Cable Line Road between Porter and Rock Springs Roads. That area was absorbed by the state park, and the houses along Cable Line Road that hadn't already been torn down were allowed to deteriorate and return to nature.

By the early 1970s, the stories of the witch's grave had become more exaggerated. It was claimed that screams could be heard at night and that the ground within the old cemetery would actually heave up and down as if the graveyard itself were breathing. Other stories told of cars not being able to start after being driven to the site. Vandalism increased at the old cemetery.

In 1972, John Lewis was a fourth grader at Highland Elementary School (now called Carlin School) in Ravenna. He recalled a day when one of his classmates brought to school a headstone with the name "Louisa Jewell" engraved upon it. This student claimed to have acquired it from the "witch's grave." The fact that it was able to be carried by a fourth-grader makes one believe that it may have been one of the smaller footstones. In any case, the site was being shown a great deal of disrespect. As for that gravestone, the last time that Lewis saw it, it was sitting in a garden in a backyard on Lafayette Avenue in Ravenna.

The story evolved slightly over the years that followed, with the addition of new aspects such as snow always melting when it came into contact with the cemetery and a suggestion that multiple witches were buried there. Authorities claimed that dozens of kids had been arrested for drug and alcohol consumption at the old cemetery. Vandalism of the headstones became more prevalent. One person even attempted to dig up a grave. By the mid-1980s, all of the tombstones were gone. Today, only a damaged sandstone wall and the base of one tombstone remain.

After the cemetery was completely destroyed and a generation or two had passed, the legend and location shifted. Sometime around 2012, a paranormal investigative team attempting to create a *Blair Witch* scenario publicized an alternate story. The new claim was that a woman was accused of practicing witchcraft during the 1800s and was executed by means of being "pressed." The practice of pressing a suspected witch was actually meant to be a form of interrogation, not execution. Pressing someone involves laying a board across their chest, then stones are placed, one by one, upon said board until the subject breaks down and confesses. A case of the use of this method was recorded during the Salem witch trials of 1692, when Giles Corey was interrogated in this manner, refused to confess and was killed when the weight became too much.

The new story of the West Branch Witch claimed that stones were placed upon the witch until she, too, was crushed under the weight. Following her death, she was buried in a remote location, and the stones used to execute her were placed in a pile upon her grave. The site of this witch's grave sits in the woods some distance to the west of the Elliott family cemetery.

One can easily find the Elliott family cemetery by entering the woods from the east end of the now-closed Cable Line Road at Porter Road. It's nestled on a ridge to the right overlooking an inlet from the Kerwin Reservoir—the same hill that Mrs. Sampson used to sled down as a child prior to the damming of the Mahoning.

In the woods to the west are a number of piles of rocks. Any one of these can be claimed as the witch's burial site. In truth, these are the ruins of farmhouses and outbuildings that are easily found on old maps.

It should be pointed out that no historical evidence exists of a witch being executed or buried in that area—not in a family cemetery, not under a pile of rocks. In short, there is no witch's grave. It's sad that all of this comes at the cost of a family's burial site.

It should be noted that the cemetery sits on park property, and the park requests that permission be granted from the park before visiting. Above all else, please be respectful. This is someone's final resting place. Furthermore, extreme caution should be exercised. As David Wright can attest, there's a high concentration of black bears and coyotes in the area. It's not advisable to go at night, as that's when many of these animals are most active. It's also advised that visitors stay on marked trails, as there are numerous hidden sinkholes.

THE CEDAR GROVE WITCH OF PENINSULA

Legends claim that Cedar Grove Cemetery, located on State Route 303 just west of Riverview Road in Peninsula, is haunted by the ghost of a wandering witch. It's said that her headstone, which bears very unusual pagan markings, has been repeatedly struck by lightning. The stone is charred and has actually melted. Only one name appears on this stone: "McGovrn."

If one would only do a little research, they would quickly discover that this "witch" isn't even a she but rather a he. His name was Robert "Bert" McGovern Jr., and by no means whatsoever was he a witch.

McGovern was born in September 1862 in Middlebury, Coventry Township, Summit County. He was one of seven children and received his education at the public school in Boston Township. By 1880, he was employed as a day laborer at a quarry near Peninsula. This was an occupation he would remain in throughout his entire working career. He never married, nor did he have any children.

Details are unclear, but sometime between 1900 and 1910, McGovern was no longer able to work, let alone support himself. It may be that he was injured in some manner during a quarrying accident. By 1910, he was living as an inmate at the Massillon State Hospital in Perry Township, Stark County. In 1920 and 1930, he resided in the Summit County Home in Munroe Falls.

McGovern passed away on April 5, 1933, at the Summit County Home. Prior to his death, Mr. McGovern employed his stone-cutting skills and carved his own cemetery monument.
It stood eight feet tall and was topped with a cross. He spelled his name at the base as it was pronounced. As for the curious marks on the monument, there are four church steeples carved into the corners and an unusual triangle on one side. Each quarryman had his own special mark—this askew triangle was McGovern's.

The only other thing that is known of McGovern is that he was regarded as something of an eccentric and that his funeral arrangements were handled by Cunningham Funeral Directors of Akron.

His headstone has been subject to much vandalism over the years—not lightning strikes, as suggested by the

Bert McGovern's monument at Cedar Grove Cemetery in Peninsula. *Photo by William G. Krejci.*

legend. People have broken off the top few feet of the monument and have even attempted to set it on fire, causing a layer of char near the top. In recent years, the stone has been cleaned and partially restored. It now stands about six feet tall, but the cross is still missing. It should further be noted that Bert McGovern is the only member of his family buried in that cemetery. Most of the others take their repose at Mt. Peace Cemetery in Akron.

The only thing about Bert McGovern that would indicate anything even remotely associated with witchcraft would be an accidental entry in the 1910 census; instead of McGovern, it names him as Bert Coven.

Some people just can't catch a break.

THE WITCH'S BALL OF VALLEY CITY

On the south side of Myrtle Hill Road in Valley City, Medina County, sits Myrtle Hill Cemetery. Also known as Hardscrabble Cemetery, this is said to be the burial place of an Ohio witch. Her grave is marked by a polished granite sphere that bears the name Stoskopf at the base.

Legends claim that the witch in question killed her sons and abusive husband by dumping arsenic into the well. After the grim deed was done, she disposed of the bodies in that well. Neighbors became suspicious and found her practicing witchcraft in the barn. Other stories say that she worked her magic in the local cemetery where she now takes her repose. Regardless of the source of the witchcraft accusations, the legends say she was put to death and buried in Myrtle Hill Cemetery with her casket placed in an upright position to prevent her from escaping the grave. Just to be certain that she couldn't get out, the large granite sphere was placed above her burial site.

Much like the stories of the West Branch Witch, rumor has it that snow refuses to stick to the monument. Other stories claim that if a brave visitor to the graveyard touches the ball and finds it warm, this is an indicator that the witch's ghost is actively roaming the cemetery.

In truth, there isn't anyone buried under the Stoskopf ball at Myrtle Hill Cemetery. This stone is a monument, not a headstone. Taking their repose beside the monument are George Stoskopf and his wife, Alma Baisch Stoskopf, and their daughter Helen S. Stoskopf Toth and her husband, Joseph Toth. George and Alma were married in 1901 by August Langhorst, an Evangelical pastor. Therefore, it would be safe to assume that they weren't witches.

The Stoskopf Ball at Myrtle Hill Cemetery in Medina County. *Photo by William G. Krejci.*

Regarding the story of a woman poisoning her family, that actually did happen in the area. Martha Hazel Wise, a widow of Albert Wise, poisoned her family with arsenic between Thanksgiving 1924 and early winter of 1925.

Various members in her immediate and extended family—seventeen in all—slowly became sick due to some unknown means. The first to die was Martha Wise's mother, Sophie Gienke Hazel, who died on December 13, 1924. Martha Wise's aunt Lillie Gienke died three weeks later on January 4, 1925. Just over a month later, Martha's uncle Fred Gienke died on February 8, 1925. Two of the Gienkes' children also took ill, and although they recovered, the poisoning had lasting effects.

Investigators knew there was more to this than a simple family illness and suspected poison. It was thought that the poison was being administered by a family member. Before long, they had a suspect. The investigators learned that Martha Wise purchased two ounces of arsenic from a local drugstore. When asked, she told the pharmacist that it was for killing rats. Wise was interrogated and finally broke down, claiming that she'd been putting it into her family's water buckets. When asked why she'd done this, she explained that she didn't know. The only thing she could add was that the devil had made her do it.

A trial was held, and Martha Hazel Wise was found guilty. She was sentenced to life in prison. Before the trial ended, the poisoning incident claimed one more victim. Edith Hazel, Martha Wise's sister-in-law, was deeply disturbed over the family deaths and committed suicide by slashing her own throat on the morning of May 7, 1925.

People blend these two seemingly unrelated stories and confuse the granite ball as being near the burial site of someone who poisoned her family. Martha Hazel Wise died in 1971 and was buried in Marysville, not at Myrtle Hill Cemetery in Valley City. Her victims, however, do take their repose in that cemetery.

Surprisingly, after doing a little research, I discovered that the stories aren't unrelated after all. One of Martha Wise's victims, her aunt Lillie Grienke, was the sister of George Stoskopf, whose grave is marked by the "witch's ball."

Ohio cemeteries close at dusk. Myrtle Hill is no exception. Visiting this cemetery after dark is illegal and a waste of time.

THE WITCH'S GRAVE OF OLMSTED FALLS

Chestnut Grove Cemetery, also known as Turkey Foot Cemetery, was established in 1855, when Oscar and Susan Kendall sold 3.52 acres of land to Olmsted Township for $200. Over the next seventy years, the cemetery slowly reached capacity. On June 5, 1925, Hannah Lewis deeded an additional 3.5 acres to the north. Eventually, a second Chestnut Grove Cemetery was established on Lewis Road just to the south of the original burial ground.

Legends of a witch's grave being located at the old cemetery have been circulating for many years. The most popular story claims that a woman was accused of witchcraft during the 1800s and was hanged from a large tree in the cemetery. After the execution, her body was cut down and buried in a grave at the base of that tree. Another tale speaks of multiple witches being buried there by fanatical townspeople who then planted the tree above their graves. One of the more obscure stories is that the witch in question was dismembered after being executed, and her dismembered body was buried in thirteen small boxes.

No one is certain how these legends began, but one theory was put forth that it originated while someone was caught in a sudden torrential downpour. As they drew closer to the grave site, the rain came down even harder. Whatever the origin of or variation on the legend, one aspect remains consistent. A visit to the witch's grave will later result in a personal tragedy.

The witch's grave was originally located within the enclosure of a small iron fence on the east side of the cemetery. The fence itself was anchored into the ground with stone blocks. The site contained no headstone, just a large tree growing in the center of the enclosure and a small dip in the ground. It was located at what was originally the far north end of the original burial ground (prior to the 1925 addition).

To discourage teenagers from going into the cemetery at night to search for the witch's grave, Olmsted Falls officials had the iron fence removed, though the stone blocks still remain at the base. It was hoped that by eliminating the fence, people would eventually forget the location. It worked, to a degree.

Since ghost hunters and legend seekers were not able to find the original site, they started exploring deeper into the cemetery. It wasn't long before they located a low-lying area close to the river in the newer section. They

These stones are all that remain of the iron fence that once surrounded the Naumann family plot at Chestnut Grove Cemetery in Olmsted Falls. *Photo by William G. Krejci.*

gathered rocks into a ring and started calling the site the "Witch's Circle." They referred to the immediately adjoining area as the "Witch's Hill."

I first heard the story of the Chestnut Grove witch's grave from my friends Sean Lavelle and Amy Mazzocco while I was still in high school. We ended up driving out there in the rain on my eighteenth birthday. The site wasn't very hard to locate, as the iron fence was still in place at that time. In truth, my first impression was that this fenced-in area was actually a compost pile, as there were leaves and grass clippings piled within the enclosure. Furthermore, it seemed so close to the edge of the cemetery that it was hard to believe anyone was actually buried there. It was pretty laughable to think that people were making trips out to a cemetery in Olmsted Falls to search for a compost pile. Debunking this story was going to be a breeze—or so I thought.

After searching cemetery maps and records, I learned that the lot in question, lot 48, contained one recorded burial, that of a man named John Naumann.

Naumann was born on February 7, 1818, in Hesse Darmstadt, Germany. He immigrated to the United States with his wife, Elizabeth, and their son John in the early 1850s and settled in Olmsted Falls, where he worked as a cooper. On February 28, 1854, John Naumann purchased a lot on Bradford Road (later called River Road) in Olmsted Falls. That year, he built a house upon the site. It's uncertain what became of John and Elizabeth Naumann's son, as he last appears in the 1860 census as being nine years old. It's possible that he passed away shortly after and was buried in lot 48 at Chestnut Grove. Burial records prior to 1936 are sketchy and incomplete.

John Naumann passed away on June 11, 1881, at sixty-three years of age. His burial in lot 48 is recorded, as he was the owner of that lot. Elizabeth Naumann continued to reside in her home on River Road until 1902, at which time she sold it to the Society for Christian Care of the Sick and Needy, which operated the German Hospital in Cleveland, where she moved after selling her house. She died at the German Hospital on February 22, 1907, and her funeral services were held at that facility. Though she's not listed as being interred in lot 48, her obituary states that she was buried in Olmsted Falls.

It should be noted that none of the Naumanns were witches. This should be evident enough in the fact that Elizabeth's funeral was held at a Christian facility.

Interestingly, the John Naumann house still stands at 7569 River Road. A sign in the front yard marks its historical significance. Every Halloween, the current homeowners decorate their house with an incredible display in the front yard, which has drawn media attention. The "Haunt of the Falls," as it's called, features a different family-friendly Halloween theme every October. Now that the connection to a local legend has been revealed, perhaps a witch-themed display will appear in the future.

MARY JANE'S GRAVE

A local legend in Richland County talks of the grave of a witch named Mary Jane. Many people claim that she is the origin of the legend of the famous Bloody Mary who appears in mirrors and haunts other cemeteries. In fact, the Bloody Mary of legend refers to Queen Mary I of England, not a woman buried in an Ohio cemetery.

The earliest telling says that Mary Jane was suspected of practicing witchcraft and was burned at the stake in the square in Mansfield. Another tale has her being hanged from a nearby stone railroad bridge. Later variations have her hanged from the tree that grows above her grave. The location of this supposed witch's grave is in Mount Olive Cemetery, sometimes called Tucker Cemetery. Earlier names for the burial ground were Croneis Lutheran Cemetery, McCann Farm Cemetery and Hersh Graveyard. This tiny cemetery rests on a dirt road at the south end of Tucker Road, just south of the community of Hastings in Monroe Township.

Sightings of the witch are commonplace in the old burial ground, or so the story goes. It's said that the tree at her grave bears a cross burnt into the bark as well as her initials, which occasionally have been seen to bleed. Another story states that grass refuses to grow upon the poisoned earth that holds her remains.

Where did these stories originate? According to Tom Finnerty, a former staff member at nearby Hidden Hollow Camp, this story was invented in 1963 by a counselor named John Hancock. The original tale was more involved than the one that is spun today. In the first telling by Hancock, a visitor to Mary Jane's grave was encouraged to pat her headstone in passing, otherwise her ghostly shade would come after the disrespectful individual. The story was told at Hidden Hollow Camp to get kids to go to sleep, although it's unclear if this tale had the desired effects.

The real Mary Jane buried at Mount Olive is Mary Jane Hendrickson, a daughter of William A. and Mary Ann Drake Hendrickson who was born in Washington Township, Holmes County, on September 22, 1825. She continued to reside in Holmes County until the 1850s, at which time she moved to Richland County and took up residency with her sister and brother-in-law, Sophia and Samuel Secrist. Mary Jane Hendrickson died in Hastings on March 3, 1898, and was buried with her family at Mount Olive Cemetery. Her cause of death was not being burned at the stake in Mansfield or hanged from a bridge or a tree in an old graveyard. She died from dropsy and cancer. Furthermore, she didn't practice witchcraft—she was an Evangelical Christian.

In regard to the cemetery, it should be noted that it has been the scene of assaults and acts of vandalism. This includes someone actually cutting down the tree that grew above Mary Jane Hendrickson's grave. This crime was perpetrated by a group of juveniles who, in cutting down the tree, also destroyed a number of monuments. Mary Jane Hendrickson's headstone is also missing, having been either removed by the cemetery caretaker or stolen by thieves. Still, the name does appear on a large stone in that cemetery along with ninety-five others.

Due to its remote location and history, visitation to this cemetery is strongly discouraged. Again, there's no witch buried there, so making a visit with expectations of witnessing something paranormal may be pointless.

The German Witches' Graves

In a small grove of trees surrounded by a farm field on Lipply Road near the southwest corner of Springfield Township, Mahoning County, sits the Haller Family Cemetery. Contained within the bounds of this tiny burial ground are the remains of four individuals who, legends maintain, were witches. The story states that they were burned at the stake for their practice of the dark arts and were buried in this remote location. It's further said that their spirits can be seen wandering the little cemetery and adjacent fields.

It's uncertain how or when this story originated. Most likely, someone simply came across the small burial ground that contains headstones with writings in German and took the words to be curses and warnings. Ignorance seems to be a major factor in the origins of witch legends. The West Branch Witch story is a perfect example of this.

Jacob Haller was born in 1797 in Hemmingen, Neckarkreis, Wuerttemberg, Germany. He settled on a 150-acre tract on what is now

Lipply Road and was married to Agnes Lipply. Three daughters were born to the couple: Katharina, Caroline and Leah. In early 1849, Katharina married an Evangelical Lutheran minister named Carl Gustav Wilhelm Sigelen. One year earlier, Reverend Carl Sigelen came to Columbiana County to take charge of the German Lutheran mission. The young Katharina Haller and her family were likely members of that congregation.

The first tragedy to strike the Haller family came with the death of Jacob and Agnes's daughter Leah, who passed away on May 20, 1849, at age thirteen. The following day, death again visited the family and claimed the life of seventeen-year-old Katharina Haller Sigelen. Both girls were laid to rest among a stand of trees upon the Haller family farm. A terrible cholera epidemic was sweeping across the state, and this may have been the cause of their deaths.

Agnes Lipply Haller died on November 2, 1873, and was laid to rest beside her daughters. Jacob Haller joined them on September 27, 1877.

As the legends of the German witches' graves spread, the cemetery started to draw curiosity and thrill seekers. Unfortunately, it also drew thieves and vandals. At least one of the headstones and some of the footstones have been stolen. Also, a large monument has been knocked off its base.

The vandalized Haller family cemetery in Mahoning County. *Photo by William G. Krejci.*

Today, the property is owned by Terry Lipply, who is a great-great-great-grandson of Agnes Lipply Haller's brother, Christian Lipply. The cemetery has been in this family since it was established in the 1840s. He strongly requests that people stay out of his ancestors' burial site. They weren't witches; they were Lutherans.

If anyone is still suspect of what's written on the most distinguishable headstone (Katharina's), in English, it reads:

> *Katharina*
> *Wife of the Evangelical Lutheran*
> *Preacher C. G. W. Sigelen*
> *she was born on the 1ˢᵗ March 1832*
> *and she died 21ˢᵗ May 1849*

The verses that appear below it, which are also written in German, are Philippians 3:20–21 and I Thessalonians 4:13–14. They're not hexes or curses—in fact, they're quite the opposite.

The Bowman Cemetery Witch

In 1813, brothers James and Benjamin Hambleton traveled to Ohio from Solebury, Bucks County, Pennsylvania, and settled in the northern part of St. Clair Township, Columbiana County, where they established themselves on three hundred acres along the Little Beaver Creek. That same year, they dug a millrace and erected a stone gristmill. In 1834, construction began on the Sandy and Beaver Canal, a seventy-three-mile-long waterway that stretched from Bolivar, Ohio, to Glasgow, Pennsylvania. The canal was set to pass right through the Hambleton property. They seized the opportunity and established the village of Sprucevale between the new canal and Little Beaver Creek, right beside their mill.

The canal was completed in 1847 and had over ninety locks. Unfortunately, the Sandy and Beaver Canal failed in 1852, when the upstream Cold Run Reservoir Dam broke and washed away much of the earthworks, locks and feeders. By 1870, Sprucevale was a ghost town. Today, only small traces remain, including some of the locks (which are discussed later in this book) and Hambleton's Mill, which is said to be haunted by a witch.

The story says that Esther Hale was a Quaker preacher who lost her soldiering husband during the Civil War. Somewhere in the grief, she also lost her mind and turned to witchcraft. Legends claim that she sacrificed children in the Bowman Cemetery and either hanged herself from a large tree or was hanged by angry neighbors in that same cemetery. Following her death, she was buried where her body dropped. Another story claims she was a jilted bride-to-be whose remains were found in her cabin after the supposed wedding never occurred.

Her ghost has been seen haunting three places. The Bowman Cemetery is the most obvious of these. The others are Hambleton's Mill in the ghost town of Sprucevale and the Echo Dell Road bridge over Little Beaver Creek. Why she would haunt the old mill is anyone's guess. It's nearly six miles from Bowman Cemetery. The Echo Dell Road bridge is a little closer, being three miles from the cemetery.

Bowman Cemetery sits in the woods on the west side of Lusk-Lock Road, just north of Middle Beaver Road and southeast of the village of Elkton. Most of the cemetery has been destroyed by witch fanatics and vandals, who have visited a fair amount of destruction upon the site. Broken headstones, candles, headless dolls and trinkets can be found just about everywhere. As far as cemetery desecration goes, this has to be the most despicable I have ever seen. At least the headstones are still present, unlike in the Elliott family cemetery.

So, now the question is: Who *really* was Esther Hale?

According to Quaker meeting records, there was a woman named Esther Pyle who married Joseph Hale in nearby Salem on November 26, 1846. In 1850, they were living in the village of Unity with a one-year-old son named Henry. By 1860, the family had moved to Indiana, where Joseph died in 1887 and Esther died in 1898. They're both buried in that state; therefore, this can't be the Esther Hale of Bowman Cemetery legend.

Another Esther Hale shows up in the 1860 census as a six-year-old daughter of Robert and Caroline Hale in Salem. She married a man named Addison H. Fritchman in 1897. She was living too late to be the woman in this legend. Also, she wasn't a Quaker.

Regarding someone in the area named Hale who died during the Civil War, we find Sergeant Thomas Teegarden Hale, a son of Warrick L. and Lucinda R. Hale. He's buried at Hope Cemetery in Salem. Sergeant Hale served with the 65th Ohio Volunteer Infantry, Company B, and died at the Battle of Stone River in Murfreesboro, Tennessee. There are two problems—Thomas Hale wasn't married, nor was he a Quaker.

Hambleton's Mill at Sprucevale, where "Esther Hale" is said to appear. *Photo by William G. Krejci.*

After completely scratching the idea that Esther Hale lost her love in the Civil War, it wasn't long before she finally turned up in my research. The Esther referred to in this legend was actually Esther *Hole*, the wife of Charles Hole. She was born Esther Hanna, daughter of Robert and Catherine Hanna of Lynchburgh, Campbell County, Virginia, on April 10, 1792. At the time of her marriage, she lived with her parents in Middletown Township in Columbiana County. Charles was a son of Jacob and Mary Hole, of the same place, and was born on June 27, 1783, in Loudoun County, Virginia. They were married at the Society of Friends Meeting House south of Little Bull Creek on May 16, 1811, and spent the rest of their lives in Columbiana County. According to the family history:

> *Esther was a minister in the Society of Friends and traveled extensively throughout Ohio and Virginia. She was a pioneer anti-slavery advocate, laboring in this reform amongst the slave holders of Virginia. She always courteously received them and argued her cause where none but such a gentle and refined Quaker lady might dare approach a subject.*

Esther Hanna Hole died at her residence near Clarkson, Columbiana County, on December 6, 1849. Her obituary read:

> *Esther, wife of Charles Hole, a minister and member of Carmel Monthly Meeting, in the fifty-eighth year of her age. During her last sickness, which was severe, she was remarkably favored with calmness and resignation, remaining sensible to the last.*

Charles Hole died on June 23, 1854. Both were buried at the Carmel Meeting House in Columbiana County in the area now known as the East Carmel Cemetery. They were the parents of nine children.

While it's true that she was a Quaker preacher, she didn't lose her husband in a war. Why would she? Quakers are largely pacifists and conscientious objectors.

Esther Hole takes her repose in the little cemetery beside the meetinghouse where she once preached the Good Word—not in Bowman Cemetery. Unfortunately, her grave is not marked by a distinguishable stone, but there are many headstones in this cemetery with names that have washed away with the passage of time. Any one of these may mark the resting place of this brave woman who objected to slavery long before that stance was popular.

As far as Bowman Cemetery is concerned, it should be left alone. The woman named in the legend isn't even buried there. Enough damage has already been done to this burial ground, and the guilty parties should be ashamed of themselves.

REAL WITCHES' GRAVES

So, if the previous stories are nothing more than urban legends, where are the real witches' graves? History tells us that the most prominent cases of people being executed for witchcraft occurred in New England during the late seventeenth century. But what about Ohio? It seems unlikely that anyone would be accused of witchcraft in a state that wasn't settled by Europeans until the late eighteenth century—but the truth may surprise you.

Around 1805, in Bethel, Clermont County, there was a case involving two girls in the Hildebrand family who claimed to have been bewitched by an elderly widowed neighbor named Nancy Evans. Houton Clark, the justice of the peace, was summoned, and the matter was addressed. A set of scales were erected, and Nancy Evans was placed on one side. On the other side, Justice Clark placed a large Bible. The idea was that if the Bible outweighed Evans, she would be guilty of witchcraft. Justice Clark addressed her, saying:

"Nancy Evans, thou art weighed against The Bible to try thee against witchcraftery and diabolical practices."

At this, the stays were removed from beneath Nancy Evans and the Bible. Needless to say, Evans significantly outweighed the Bible, passed the test and was acquitted. Though she pitied her ignorant neighbors, subjecting herself to the test must have been too much of an embarrassment, as she moved to Hamersville, Brown County, to live with relatives, where it's presumed her grave is located.

The early nineteenth century wasn't too far removed from the era of the Salem witch trials, but one would think that by the late nineteenth century, we as a society would've moved beyond such superstitions. Not so. Interestingly, Ohio saw its own Salem witch trial in 1893, but the scenario is not what you may think.

In 1852, thirteen-year-old Jacob Culp immigrated to the United States from Germany and settled near Salem in Columbiana County. Five years later, he met a widow named Hannah Loop Walker, and the two were soon married. Unfortunately, many of Hannah's family members objected to the union, as Jacob was sixteen years younger than his wife. Otherwise, they enjoyed a marital bliss that lasted until Hannah's death in 1886 at the age of sixty-two.

Hanna's family was outraged even further when Jacob married Hannah's twenty-three-year-old niece, Hattie Loop, just ten months after his first wife's death. Particularly incensed over the marriage were Hattie's sisters Sadie, Ella and Fannie. Sadie was the most affected.

In the fall of 1892, Hattie's mother took ill. When the doctor couldn't find a cure, the family turned to spiritual healers Louisa Burns and Dr. Andrew Hoff. Hattie's mother died nonetheless, but the healers placed the blame on Hattie's husband, whom they claimed was a sorcerer who possessed dark abilities. They also claimed that he'd caused the death of his first wife.

Hattie's sister Sadie spread this rumor among the parishioners at Hart's Methodist Episcopal Church, the congregation to which the family belonged. It didn't have the desired effect. Sadie Loop was charged with falsehood. She was given the opportunity to withdraw her claim and make amends with her brother-in-law, but she refused. Thus, a trial was held at the church on May 23, 1893.

A plea of "not guilty" was entered, and witnesses were called for both sides, but the evidence against Sadie Loop was overwhelming. After ten minutes, a verdict was returned:

> *We, the committee in the case of Miss Sadie Loop, charged with falsehood under the specification that she had on or about the 27th day of April,*

1893, published contrary to the word of God and the discipline, the following false and evil matter of and concerning Jacob Culp, to-wit, that he, Jacob Culp, was a wizard and practiced witchcraft, find that said specification is proven and the charge of falsehood sustained.

Sadie Loop was expelled from the church, and that looked to be the end of it. Unfortunately, troubles continued for Jacob Culp. That fall, his brother-in-law accused him of cursing a well. The suggestion that Culp had bewitched the well came at the insistence of the previously mentioned Dr. Hoff. This accusation spread throughout the community and was supported by the rest of Culp's wife's siblings. The rest of the Loop family faced expulsion from the church.

A trial was set for January 25, 1894, but Culp's in-laws refused to show up. Nevertheless, a verdict was reached, and the accusers were excommunicated.

Jacob Culp died on May 8, 1928, and is buried at Franklin Square Cemetery in Columbiana County. His grave may not be the grave of a witch, but it is the grave of a person who was accused of witchcraft. That in itself is quite rare to see, especially in Ohio.

The only person known to have been executed for witchcraft in Ohio was the great Native American leader Leatherlips, in 1810.

Leatherlips (or Sha-Te-Yah-Ron-Ya, as he was called in his mother tongue) was a noted chief of the Porcupine Clan of the Wyandots and had signed the Treaty of Greenville following the Native American defeat at the Battle of Fallen Timbers. After signing the treaty, Leatherlips became friendly toward whites, which outraged Tecumseh, the leader of a confederation of Native Americans who were opposed to the western expansion of the United States and the forced expulsion of Native Americans.

As conflicts between the United States and Tecumseh's Confederation increased, Tecumseh sent a delegation to meet with Leatherlips in hopes of gaining his support. Leatherlips refused and sent away the delegation. On their return trip, members of this delegation fell ill and died near present-day Huron. When the survivors reached Tecumseh and relayed what had happened, Tecumseh accused Leatherlips of practicing witchcraft and cursing the delegation. An execution party was sent to carry out a sentence of death.

Leatherlips was executed by a single blow from a tomahawk to the back of the head. Though the official charge was witchcraft, Leatherlips' death was actually politically motivated. Without their leader to guide them, his people joined Tecumseh's Confederation.

The resting place of Leatherlips is not known, but it's believed to be near the Olentangy Indian Caverns north of Dublin. Not only was Leatherlips the only person executed for witchcraft in Ohio, he may have been the last person executed for witchcraft in the United States.

As far as true witches' graves are concerned, it should be concluded here that Ohio is full of them. One doesn't have to be executed for witchcraft in order to have a witch's grave. Personally speaking, I've known quite a few people who follow the beautiful practice of Wicca. Obviously, people who follow that practice have passed away and are buried in local cemeteries. I do know where a few of them are interred, but for privacy reasons, I refuse to disclose who they are and the locations of their grave sites.

CHAPTER III

RAILROAD GHOSTS

INTRODUCTION

In many cases, tales of hauntings seem to be centered around disasters. Northern Ohio has experienced no shortage of these. Rail travel in the nineteenth century was a risky thing. Construction standards were poor, and an accurate means of timekeeping was still in its infancy. In short, rail travel was a gamble, and you took your life into your hands when traveling by train.

Since there has been some confusion as to where many of these disasters have occurred, I'm including GPS coordinates to act as reference points. Please be respectful when exploring these areas, and remember that people have lost their lives at these locations. Also, active rail lines are the property of their respective railroads, and trespassing is illegal.

THE ASHTABULA BRIDGE DISASTER

41.878431, -80.789415

One of the most talked about railroad ghost stories in Northern Ohio seems to be the tale of the Ashtabula Bridge disaster. Widely regarded as the most horrific rail catastrophe the state has ever known, it was often compared with later wrecks. For those unfamiliar with this tale of woe, keep reading.

On December 29, 1876, the Lake Shore & Michigan Southern Railroad's Pacific Express No. 5 was westbound with eleven cars and two engines, the *Socrates* and the *Columbia*. The train was loaded with nearly 160 passengers, and a terrible snowstorm had kicked up. At 7:28 p.m., the train decelerated while approaching the station at Ashtabula and slowly crossed the iron bridge over the Ashtabula River.

Just as the *Socrates* reached the west end of the span, there was a loud crashing sound as the bridge collapsed, and the *Columbia* and passenger cars plunged into the icy river. Oil from the lanterns spilled everywhere, and when it met with the wood-burning stoves, it turned the crushed wooden passenger cars into an inferno.

Those who weren't killed in the initial plummet were burned or drowned. In the end, ninety-two people lay dead and sixty-four were injured. Of the dead, forty-eight were completely unrecognizable and were buried in a mass grave at nearby Chestnut Grove Cemetery. A large monument was placed at the grave site nineteen years later.

Scene of the Ashtabula Bridge disaster on the morning of December 30, 1876. *Courtesy Ashtabula Public Library.*

A burned needlework textile recovered from the wreckage of the Ashtabula Bridge disaster. This textile and other artifacts are in the hands of the Ashtabula Public Library. *Photo by William G. Krejci.*

An investigation followed, after which it was determined that the cause of the disaster was the bridge itself, citing poor construction standards and a lack of proper maintenance. Charles Collins, the engineer in charge of the bridge's maintenance, was widely ridiculed afterward. Twenty days after the accident, he was found dead in his bedroom. His death was originally ruled a suicide, but a year and a half later, the ruling was changed to homicide. His killer was never identified.

One who did actually kill himself was Amasa Stone, the president of the railroad that built the bridge. A little over six years later, he shot himself through the heart.

As far as the haunting is concerned, most of the events are experienced at Chestnut Grove Cemetery, where the unidentified victims are buried. Also buried there is Collins, whose mausoleum is just feet away from the mass burial site of the victims of the bridge disaster. The ghost of Collins, as well as those of a number of other people in mid-1870s attire, have been sighted roaming the cemetery grounds.

Many people claim that the disaster site itself is not haunted. However, there have been many claims of ghostly figures walking about the site, especially around the time of the anniversary of the tragedy, when the river is covered in ice.

THE REPUBLIC HORROR

41.121529, -83.034566

Around 2:30 in the morning on January 4, 1887, the Baltimore & Ohio Express No. 5, a fast-moving passenger train from New York to Chicago, collided with an eastbound freight train on a bend just west of the small town of Republic. The passenger train, which was traveling at sixty-three miles per hour, consisted of five coaches (one of which was a smoking car), four sleepers and a luggage car, and the train was filled with post-holiday travelers.

As the passenger train rounded the bend, the engineer saw the freight train, applied the brakes, reversed the engine and jumped for his life. Three seconds later, the two trains met in a horrible collision that newspapers dubbed the "Republic Horror."

The coach cars telescoped into one another, while the sleepers were spared any serious injury. Almost instantly, fire broke out in the smoking car and quickly spread. Many passengers were killed outright, while others who were trapped in the mangled wreck slowly burned to death.

The freight train was making the run from the Seneca siding to the one at Republic—a distance of five miles—when the engine ran out of steam and stalled on the line. No flag or warning lantern was sent ahead to indicate that the track was being blocked by the stopped train. The crew of the freight train survived by jumping out and running before the express reached them. It was ultimately determined that the crew members on the freight train were intoxicated, having been spotted at saloons in Fostoria and Bloomdale earlier that day.

Sadly, the number of people killed in this disaster was never determined. Some estimates place the death toll at close to twenty-two souls. The charred and unidentified remains were taken to the undertaker's in Republic and, after a few days, buried in a mass grave.

Exactly two months later, a ghostly apparition started to make its presence known at Republic. On three occasions, the phantom figure of a woman in white, holding a lantern shining a red light, was witnessed standing along the side of the tracks. Upon seeing the warning signal, the conductor of the B&O Express No. 5, following the same schedule as its ill-fated predecessor, applied the brakes and reversed the engine, bringing the train to a standstill at the exact site of the Republic Horror. Upon investigating the tracks ahead, the engineer could see no evidence of an obstruction on the line, nor could

Above: A view of the wreckage at Republic, circa 1887. *Courtesy Seneca County Museum.*

Left: The viaduct just east of Republic. *Courtesy Seneca County Museum.*

he or the fireman locate the mysterious woman who'd signaled them to stop. Even the operator at the Republic station had no answers.

In recent years, there have been claims that the ghost of the train itself has been witnessed along that stretch of track crossing the trestle approaching the site of the wreck. Interestingly, there's no trestle near Republic. There is, however, a viaduct just east of town that's said to be haunted by the ghost of its builder.

In that story, the engineer on the viaduct project was said to have made a critical blunder. There are two passageways beneath the viaduct. One arch is for Rock Creek, and the other is for South Madison Street. It's said that the wider of these two was supposed to be for the road, while the narrower one was to be used for the creek. Any visitor to the site will see that this is not the case. The story claims that the builder, upon realizing his error, hanged himself from the viaduct, though no evidence exists to support this story. Just north of this viaduct sits Farewell Retreat Cemetery, where the unidentified victims of the Republic Horror are buried.

GHOSTLY WAILS AT THE FRONT AVENUE CROSSING

41.500926, -81.705087

In the early months of 1910, employees of the Cleveland, Columbus, Cincinnati & St. Louis Railroad (a.k.a. the Big Four Railroad) were being terrified by the sounds of some unseen spirit. The noise, which was described as sounding like the moans and wails of a person in the agony of death, was heard every Sunday around midnight near the Front Avenue crossing and Big Four freight depot in Cleveland. The initial reports, which made the newspapers on February 14 of that year, were made by flagman Michael Weir, watchman Joe Domley and telephone operator May Murphy. After many weeks, two investigating railroad policemen named Frank Kennedy and Jess Millward were baffled over the origin of the noise. It was widely believed that the site was being haunted by the ghost of an ore dock worker who'd been cut down by a train at the crossing the previous December.

One week after the story was made public, flagman Weir assembled a large group of men at the site to listen for the sound. As expected, the wailing was heard just before midnight, at which time the group disbanded and hastily retreated home.

Three days later, newspapers reported that the source had been discovered, but reports were contradictory as to who was making the noises. One source stated that it was someone trying to frighten flagman Weir, while another reported, quite absurdly, that it was the handiwork of a vaudeville ventriloquist in training. No solid cause was revealed.

It should be noted that less than a month and a half later, forty-six-year-old baggage handler Peter Keenan was struck and killed at the Front Avenue crossing. His fragmented remains were discovered by a Big Four Railroad switchman.

These events occurred on the east bank of the flats where the RTA Waterfront Line now crosses Front Avenue between West 10th and West 11th Streets.

ARCADIA'S HEADLESS GHOST

41.103486, -83.530929

Located in the northeast part of Hancock County is the village of Arcadia, where a headless ghost is said to roam. Most legends state that a man named Jimmie Welsh was beheaded while working on the railroad in that area and that his ghost continues to wander in search of its missing head. The true facts of the story are quite sad but have spawned a ghostly tale that has endured for over a century.

John H. Welsh was born in 1867 to Irish-born parents Lawrence and Mary Tivenen Welsh. The oldest of five children, John was raised in Dalton City, Illinois, where his father worked as a section boss on the railroad. In 1887, John Welsh moved with his brother William to Lima, where they boarded in the home of a woman named Mrs. Throckmorton at 255 South Main Street. It was at that point that the boys found employment with the Lake Erie & Western Railroad. William worked in the Lima yard, while John was employed as a conductor.

At 12:15 a.m. on October 2, 1889, LE&W freight train No. 44 was eastbound but had stopped just southwest of Arcadia. Northeast of town, the LE&W tracks crossed over those of the Nickel Plate Railroad, where another train on that line was passing. While waiting for the Nickel Plate train to clear the line, conductor John Welsh noticed that a portion of his train had become uncoupled. At this, he jumped from the locomotive and made his way to the rear of the separated cars to apply the brakes so that the engineer could slowly back up and reconnect the train. As he was setting the brake on an oil tank car, another separated section of train came rolling toward him and smashed into the car on which he was standing. His head was caught between the two cars, and the top of his skull was horrifically crushed. His body remained wedged for the next four hours until a wrecking train arrived. Nine cars were totally destroyed in the wreck, and it was many hours before the line was cleared.

John Welsh's body was returned to Dalton City by his brother William, and he was buried there. John H. Welsh was twenty-two years old.

The story of the haunting first appeared in the *Toledo Blade* on the evening of January 14, 1890, as a special from Findlay. By the following morning, the sensational tale was making its way into newspapers across the country. It stated:

Trainmen on the Lake Erie & Western Railroad, between Findlay and Fostoria and greatly disturbed over, what they claim, is the ghost of a dead freight conductor, who was killed one night last November, about 8 miles east of this city, by his train breaking into two sections, and then coming together suddenly, throwing the conductor from the car on which he was standing to the tracks below, where he was beheaded by the wheels before the train could be controlled.

This accident occurred near the village of Arcadia, at a point where dense woods almost form an arch above the tracks; and here it is that the ghost of Jimmie Welsh, the mutilated conductor, makes its appearance nearly every night, as the midnight passenger train from Sandusky going west reaches the spot where he met his fate on that gloomy, autumnal night less than three months ago.

The engineer and other officials of the train assert that scarcely a night passes, but what a headless apparition can be seen coming out of these woods, as the train nears the scene of the accident, carrying in its bloodless hand, something that looks like a lantern, which it waves backward and forward in a measureless sort of manner, as if searching for a lost object. The trainmen have no sort of doubt but it is the ghost of Jimmie Welsh, hunting for its head. The phantom is plainly visible until the engine, with a scream of terror, voicing the feelings of the engineer, endeavors to escape from the horrible sight, when it slowly turns, and walking into the woods fades away into a blue mist.

It was further stated that the headless spirit only appeared to that late-night train and had caused entire crews to abandon the shift. A conductor and brakeman on the train confirmed the story, stating that the ghost would be less pronounced on moonlit nights, while it was more visible on dark or rainy nights.

It should be noted that until this story of the haunting appeared in the papers, conductor Welsh's first name was John. He's been mistakenly called Jimmie ever since. The article also states that the tragedy happened in November, while in reality, it occurred in October. Also, John Welsh wasn't decapitated by the wheels of his train, as this story suggests.

THE SPRIGHTLY SPECTER OF CONNEAUT

41.951379, -80.547497

An article in the *Cleveland Plain Dealer* from February 1891 reported on what it called a "sprightly ghost" making its presence known in Conneaut, near Ashtabula. The specter was witnessed by many people the previous fall and early winter. It was said to be a ghastly, frightful figure, which primarily haunted a boathouse on the bank of Conneaut Creek, a few rods above the stone arched viaduct of the Lake Shore & Michigan Southern Railroad.

The author of the article ascribed the identity of the ghost as being the spirit of a handsome and clever young man named Woodward who had died at the site of the boathouse some twenty-four years earlier while attempting to cross the creek. After stepping into a skiff and untying

the line, the man suffered a seizure, fell into the creek and drowned in less than three feet of water. Since that unfortunate event, people had avoided the area, but those who happened onto the spot sometimes witnessed disturbances on the water and, later, strange noises coming from the boathouse.

It wasn't until the fall of 1890 that the ghost began to wander beyond its original haunt. Almost nightly, people saw it walking along the railroad tracks or ascending the bank from the creek flats below the viaduct. It was said to be carrying a large, partially concealed lantern. Its head was thrown back, eyes partly closed, and its respiration was accompanied by a gurgling sound, as if it were attempting to expel water from its nasal passage.

Henry Woodworth's headstone at Conneaut Cemetery. The image engraved at the top is of a rowboat. *Photo by William G. Krejci.*

Upon looking into the story of Mr. Woodward, it became clear that the man's name was actually Woodworth. His death also occurred much earlier than the newspaper article stated.

Henry Woodworth was born in 1835 to Elijah and Edna Ferris Woodworth. The tragedy in question struck on the morning of May 2, 1856. Henry was fishing on the creek, and according to his obituary, it was believed he'd suffered a fit while exiting his skiff. His body was found in the water that afternoon near an old steam mill on the creek. From all appearances, he died without struggle. Henry Woodworth was twenty-one years old.

Henry's father, Elijah, was so upset by the death of his son that it was said he lamented the young man's passing with great pain. When Elijah died in 1900, his obituary said:

> *When a beloved son was drowned in one of the lower reaches of the creek, the father was broken with grief, and a carving over the son's grave in Conneaut Cemetery pathetically attests both his affection and his affliction. All the more touching is the tribute because it is so inartistic and so ghostly.*

THE KIPTON COLLISION

41.267386, -82.305108

Two and a half months after the report of the ghost at Conneaut haunting the viaduct of the Lake Shore & Michigan Southern Railroad, a terrible disaster occurred on that same rail line in the village of Kipton in Lorain County.

The afternoon of April 18, 1891, was bright and beautiful and seemed to be a perfect spring day for traveling. The westbound LS&MS Toledo Express No. 21, a passenger train, pulled up to the old wooden station at Kipton, much to the shock and concern of the telegraph operator. The train should have stopped at a siding at Oberlin four miles to the east. Realizing the severity of the situation, the operator turned for the signal to warn other trains that the tracks were not clear of traffic, as they should have been, but it was too late. A moment later, the eastbound fast-mail train No. 14 thundered into view and, at a speed of fifty miles per hour, collided head-on with No. 21. The station then became the scene of the worst disaster that railroad had seen since the Ashtabula Bridge disaster of 1876.

The wreckage at Kipton in 1891. *Oberlin Heritage Center. Oberlin, Ohio.*

In the end, eight people lay dead, and six others were severely injured. Killed in the wreck were the engineers of both locomotives and six postal clerks from the No. 14. It was determined that the conductor's watch on the No. 21 had stopped working or was running slow. This prompted the government to hire Cleveland watchmaker Webb C. Ball to set the standard for all railroad watches. Some have suggested that this is where the phrase "get on the ball" originated, while others claim that the term relates to sports.

Today, the site of the wreck is located in Kipton Community Park and is marked with an Ohio Historical Marker.

Stories of the site being haunted are relatively new and don't appear to predate 2015. These recent tales mention ghostly sightings along the bicycle path that follows the old railroad route from Elyria west to the county line. Ghost walks have been conducted at the site, and it's become a popular stop for local ghost-hunting groups.

DEATH ON THE DOODLEBUG

41.147485, -81.472104

Cuyahoga Falls saw its worst rail disaster on the evening of July 31, 1940. The Doodlebug No. 4648 was a one-car, gasoline-electric passenger trolley that serviced the Pennsylvania Railroad. Originally steam-powered, it was brought to Akron in 1918 and was one of a few such trolleys that made the run.

On the evening of the disaster, the Doodlebug was making the run from Hudson to Akron with forty-three passengers, a conductor, an engineer and a Pennsylvania Railroad employee, who was riding in the baggage compartment. It was traveling at thirty miles per hour when it reached the outskirts of Cuyahoga Falls. At 5:58 p.m., it rolled through the Front Street crossing. A moment later, a two-engine, seventy-three-car freight train rounded the bend at the Cuyahoga River and collided head-on with the Doodlebug. The crew of the little commuter car had only a moment to react and jumped for their lives. So severe was the impact that the leading locomotive telescoped itself twelve feet into the Doodlebug, rupturing the 350-gallon gasoline tank and causing a massive explosion. The flaming wreckage was pushed five hundred feet backward across the Front Street crossing until it finally came to rest between the crossings at Hudson Drive and Second Street.

The Doodlebug collision at Cuyahoga Falls, circa 1940. *Courtesy Cuyahoga Falls Historical Society.*

At once, a large crowd assembled at the scene to lend assistance, but with the flames being so intense, no one could get close enough to help. All forty-three passengers were killed. According to Coroner R.E. Amos, only nine of the victims died in the initial impact. The rest burned to death.

During an investigation into the disaster, it was learned that the Doodlebug should've taken the siding at Silver Lake to let the freight train pass, but for some reason, it continued on. Its engineer, Thomas Leo Murtaugh, had no memory of passing the Silver Lake siding. He'd been complaining to the railroad about a strong gasoline odor in the cab, and it was determined that Murtaugh was disoriented by gasoline fumes from a leaking fuel tank.

The Doodlebug disaster prompted the installation of an automatic signal system on that rail line that was decidedly more efficient than the old system, which consisted of handing the engineer a slip of paper that told him when and where to meet oncoming rail traffic.

The last Doodlebug made its final Akron run exactly eleven years to the day after the disaster.

As with the Kipton collision, ghost stories concerning the Doodlebug disaster are a recent development, with people making claims of seeing ghostly passengers walking along the old rail line. As of late, the site has become popular among amateur paranormal investigators.

In truth, it's impossible to know who, if anyone, haunts the site. Prior to 1940, the Front Street crossing was the scene of numerous grade-crossing fatalities. The worst of these involved the deaths of three young men from Portage County who drove their car into the side of a locomotive tender on the night of October 10, 1933.

While ghost stories involving the Doodlebug don't predate 2012, there are two other tales from the immediate area that go back over one hundred years.

THE ALPHABET RAILROAD POWERHOUSE

41.147350, -81.472813

Just two hundred feet to the west of the Doodlebug disaster site, across Hudson Drive and just south of Second Street, sat the powerhouse for the Alphabet Railroad. The Akron, Bedford & Cleveland Railroad (a.k.a. the ABC or Alphabet Railroad) began service in 1895 and was the world's longest electric railroad. Around 1900, it merged with several other railroads and became part of the Northern Ohio Traction & Light Company, which discontinued passenger service in the early 1930s. Today, the old route of the Alphabet Railroad is used by the RTA rapid Blue Line in Cleveland and Shaker Heights, then travels south toward Akron along what is now State Route 8.

In late January 1896, reports were made regarding a haunting at the Alphabet Railroad powerhouse in Cuyahoga Falls. At around 2:30 in the morning, a ghostly white figure would appear at various locations in and around the powerhouse. On Friday, January 24, the powerhouse staff made a decision to investigate the matter. Motorman Frank Bliler was stationed in the engine room. Right on schedule, Bliler heard someone walking across the room and turned just in time to see a white object enter a small closet. Without taking his eyes from the closet door, he called out to the engineer, fireman and night watchman, who came up and surrounded the door. Upon throwing it open, they found the closet empty. Almost at once, they heard a scream from behind them and turned to see the white phantom, its arms outstretched, standing across the room. In an instant, it sank into the floor. The screams and screeches continued, but the ghost did not reappear that night.

The following evening, another group kept vigil, and at 2:30 a.m., the ghostly visitor returned. Footsteps were heard from above, as if someone were walking across the boilers. A ladder was set up, and one of the men ascended. Upon reaching the top of the boilers, a wall of fire shot up before him. He quickly climbed back down and did not attempt to investigate further.

Someone who doubted the haunting was a car inspector named Murray DeFrance. Resolved to get to the bottom of the matter, he decided that he'd stay alone in the powerhouse one night. Shortly after two in the morning, he was roused by the sound of groans and screams coming from outside. He ran out, and there, atop the coal pile, he saw the white object fluttering about as if being blown around by a strong wind, though the night was calm and still. Satisfied that the site was haunted, DeFrance made his escape as hastily as possible.

Some believe that the appearances of certain ghosts may be a warning of disasters to come, which might have been the case with the Alphabet Railroad Powerhouse ghost.

On the night of September 29, 1905, a flywheel at the powerhouse that weighed twenty-two tons disintegrated and flew to pieces, tearing holes through the walls and roof of the building. Some pieces that weighed as

Workmen at the Alphabet Railroad Powerhouse in 1895. *Courtesy Cuyahoga Falls Historical Society.*

much as two tons were thrown more than two hundred yards through the air, landing on a nearby saloon, hotel, the car barns for the electric railroad and a potato garden. The cause of this was a failed control governor. Miraculously, no one was severely injured.

The other ghostly legend of the area involves a headless ghost near the river.

On the night of April 13, 1853, James Parks and William Beatson were observed drinking heavily in Akron and at Hall's Tavern in Cuyahoga Falls. After imbibing to excess at Hall's and being denied further drinks, the two left the tavern. Beatson was so intoxicated that he left his coat behind. The drunken men made their way toward the river. From there, the story turns tragic.

According to Parks, they attempted to cross the river on the stone railroad bridge, but upon stepping out onto the span, the two men fell between the ties and landed on the road below. Parks searched through the darkness for his companion and soon found him to be deceased. As it was, Parks had a long criminal past. He knew for certain that he'd be accused of murder. At this, he decided to remove William Beatson's clothes to hide the man's identity. Not satisfied that this would suffice, he pulled out his knife and removed Beatson's head. The headless body was dumped in the river, and his clothes were later tossed into the canal.

Shortly after daybreak, the bloody scene on the road beneath the railroad viaduct and beside the river told of the violence that occurred there only a few hours earlier. Blood was splattered about the area, and Beatson's cane and vest were discovered nearby. A day later, the headless body was found about thirty feet from the bridge. His head has never been recovered.

Parks made his way to Cleveland and, from there, to Buffalo, where he was arrested and returned to Ohio. James Parks, whose real name was James Dickenson, was tried and convicted for the murder of William Beatson. Evidence was given that Beatson was beaten with a rock and stabbed in the neck while still alive. According to the prosecution, the motive for the crime was robbery, as Beatson had been carrying a large sum of money on him. Parks went to the gallows at Cleveland on June 1, 1855. He maintained his innocence to the end.

It's been recorded through oral tradition that a ghostly apparition, lacking a cranium, has been seen in an overcoat, carrying a cane and wandering around the area where William Beatson took his last breath. Like the storied "Jimmie" Welsh, Beatson's restless spirit is also said to be searching for his missing head, although he seemed to have recovered his coat and cane.

The site of Beatson's death is at the approach beneath the old railroad line, where Bailey Road once crossed the river. This was determined by the blood and Beatson's personal effects being discovered there. Curiously, it sits exactly one hundred feet to the east of a monument to the victims of the Doodlebug collision that was dedicated in 2005.

CHAPTER IV

CRYBABY BRIDGES

THE STORIED BRIDGES

The legend of the "crybaby bridge" isn't strictly limited to Northern Ohio. It seems that the first crybaby bridge story appeared in print in the mid-1970s, and the bridge was located on Dunlap Roddey Road a few miles south of Rock Hill, South Carolina. It's possible that similar stories existed earlier, but as far as being the first to make the newspaper, the Rock Hill bridge gets the credit.

Virginia, Maryland, Oklahoma and Texas are also supposed sites of crybaby bridges. As far as Ohio is concerned, the first reported bridge of this type is located in Rogues' Hollow outside of Doylestown. The story of that bridge, which crosses Silver Creek near the Chidester Mill, is fairly recent and first appeared in the early 1980s. It wasn't even mentioned in the book *The History and Legends of Rogues' Hollow*, which was released in 1958. If this were a historic ghost story, the book's author would've included it, as he included every other ghost story from that location.

The tale of the crybaby bridge is a distressing one, and the reader should be warned that it involves unsettling stories of infanticide. Please read this chapter with a stout heart. The story, in brief, typically goes like this: Back in the early 1800s, there was a woman who had a child out of wedlock. Facing shame and ridicule from her neighbors, she stole away with her unwanted child to a nearby bridge and threw it into the river. In some

The Egypt Road Bridge in Salem. *Photo by William G. Krejci.*

variations of this story, the mother throws herself in after her child. Other stories say that the mother was a runaway slave and threw her child into the river to prevent it from being captured by slave hunters. More recent tellings claim that the child was killed in an automobile accident on the bridge in question.

The stories related to each site seem to be irrelevant. They all end in the same manner, stating that those who visit these bridges at night hear the sounds of a child's cry. Thus, they've been dubbed crybaby bridges.

It should be noted that it must have been very difficult to be a child in the 1800s, what with all of these mothers throwing their children from bridges. If even half of these stories bear a shred of historic truth, the mortality rate of children being murdered by their mothers would be astronomical. Though many are claimed, the most notable of the Northern Ohio crybaby bridges are the Main Street Bridge in Clinton, the Dean Road Bridge near Wakeman, the Egypt Road Bridge in Salem, the Greely Chapel Road Bridge in Lima, the Palmer Road Bridge in Mendon, the Gore Orphanage Road Bridge in Brownhelm and the Wisner Road Bridge in Chardon. Also included in this list is the previously mentioned bridge in Boston. In many cases, an urban legend has some basis in truth, yet no evidence exists to support a story of infanticide ever having occurred at any of these sites.

OTHER HAUNTED CROSSINGS

A couple of other tales that seem to run hand in hand with legendary crybaby bridge are the stories of the Elmore Rider and the Screamy Mimi Bridge.

The Elmore ghost story is one that's been told many times and in relation to many other locations. In this tale, a soldier returned home to Elmore in Ottawa County following the end of World War I. Before he left for the war, he'd proposed to his sweetheart, who'd promised that she'd wait for him. When he returned home after the war, he purchased a motorcycle and drove to the home of his affianced. As he approached the house, he saw her through the large front window in the arms of another man. In a state of despair, he turned around and sped away, and as he approached a bridge near the bottom of a hill, he lost control of his motorcycle and wrecked into the side of the bridge. He was most frightfully decapitated in the accident. A similar story claims that a wire was strung across the road near the bridge by practical jokers. The result is still the same.

It's said that if someone drives out to that bridge at night and parks their car, followed by flashing the headlights three times, the "spooklight" of the motorcyclist's headlight is supposed to appear, coming down the hill. As the light reaches the bridge, it's said that the rider is visibly without his head. In an instant, the rider and ghostly cycle vanish into nothingness.

Many cities claim this headless biker story (or some variation of it) as their own, and Elmore is no exception. No evidence exists to support the story of a man being decapitated while riding his motorcycle in Elmore.

The story of the Screamy Mimi bridge, also called the *Screaming* Mimi bridge, is, by comparison, a very different story. In that tale, Mimi was the daughter of a rich family. She'd recently married a gold-digger who was only interested in her inheritance. It's said that he murdered her at the site of a bridge and threw her dismembered body into the river. Just as with the Elmore Rider, flashing your headlights three times at night will summon the angry ghost of Mimi.

The name "Screaming Mimi" first appeared as the title of a pulp novel by Fredric Brown in 1949. Nine years later, it was adapted into a film directed by Gerd Oswald.

The site of the Screamy Mimi bridge is on Dunkard Church Road over Sugar Creek in rural Seneca County. As with the Elmore Rider and the previously mentioned crybaby bridges, no evidence exists to support the Screamy Mimi legend.

ACTUAL INCIDENTS

This is not to say that tragedies have never occurred at bridges that are said to be haunted. Three of the crossings said to be crybaby bridges were the scenes of terrible tragedies. The first is the old covered bridge at Newton Falls. Just as is the case with most crybaby bridges, the one at Newton Falls was said to involve a mother throwing her child over the side in the 1800s. Like the covered bridge at Boston, the one at Newton Falls has closed sides, making it impossible for anyone to throw anything over the side. The bridge, which was erected in 1831, is the oldest in the state of Ohio that still carries traffic. A covered sidewalk, which runs along the side of the bridge, was added in 1921.

The true tragedy of the Newton Falls covered bridge occurred on August 14, 1871. A man named Fuller had brought a load of milk to a nearby cheese factory. After unloading, he was preparing to depart when his team of two horses was startled and took off at a high rate of speed toward the bridge. At the same time, a man named Christopher Lee was crossing the bridge in his buggy with his twenty-five-year-old daughter Celia. A collision occurred halfway across the bridge. Lee's horse was impaled by the tongue of Mr. Fuller's wagon, and all three horses came crashing down on the Lees, completely destroying their buggy and burying them under the horses and debris. Lee's horse died within minutes. Celia Lee died of her injuries a few days later.

The covered bridge at Newton Falls. *Photo by William G. Krejci.*

Tindall Bridge in Fremont, where Samuel Tannyhill murdered Shirley Bradford in 1955. *Photo by William G. Krejci.*

Another noted crybaby bridge is located on Abbeyville Road near Valley City. Again, it is part of the story of a mother discarding her child in a horrible manner. While no evidence exists to support that story, a September 1898 incident involved a runaway team of horses and a party of eight young people returning home. The story states that the frightened passengers jumped from the speeding wagon. In doing so, twenty-one-year-old Anna Gollmar broke her neck and was instantly killed.

The last of these bridges that carries the legend is the Tindall Bridge near Fremont. The first bridge at Tindall's Mill was built in 1864 by J.P. Elderkin for $5,000. That bridge stood upon the site until it was washed away in the great flood of 1913. It was rebuilt by the Champion Iron Company and the Croghan Construction Company at a cost of $15,000. During construction, the bridge was twice washed out by floods. It finally opened in September 1916 and, due to its recent troubles, was referred to as the Hard Luck Bridge.

The real tragedy at the Tindall Bridge occurred on May 2, 1955. In the early morning hours, Samuel Woodrow Tannyhill went to the Hut Restaurant in Fremont and robbed the place at gunpoint. The only person in the restaurant was Shirley Bradford. After Bradford gave him the money from the register, Tannyhill forced her into his car and drove her to the Tindall Bridge, where he beat her to death with the handle of his tire jack. Tannyhill was executed on November 26, 1956, in the electric chair at the Ohio Penitentiary.

TRUE CASES

When researching this subject, I wondered if mothers had ever killed their children in the manner described in the crybaby bridge legend. In most cases, mothers who committed infanticide had done so by drowning their child in a cistern or well located on their own property. In May 1861, thirty-year-old Maria Kerg, who felt that her reputation had been damaged beyond repair by neighbors who'd accused her of theft, killed her infant daughter by throwing her into the cistern in the backyard. Immediately after, Kerg threw herself in. Both she and her daughter were discovered by her horrified husband a little over an hour later. The location of this cistern in now the back parking lot of the former bank building on the southwest corner of Lorain Avenue and West 25th Street in Cleveland. Curiously, there are few reports of cries being heard coming from old wells or cisterns.

Aside from that sad tale, there are quite a few unsolved cases of infanticide that really did involve bridges. On the morning of April 14, 1851, the body of an infant female was found in the canal at the upper bridge in Cleveland. The child had been thrown into the water within a few hours of its birth and was in the water for only a short time.

On September 4, 1865, a newborn male infant was found floating in the Cuyahoga River near the Lighthouse Street Bridge. A string was tightly tied about the child's throat, and no perpetrator was ever discovered. The identity of the child is still unknown. His remains were buried at Erie Street Cemetery in Section 10, Alley 9, Grave 58. The burial information simply states that the boy was found in the river.

On the afternoon of Wednesday, May 8, 1868, the body of a newborn male infant was found in the Sandusky River a short distance below Fremont. He had a stone tied to his neck with a piece of string about two or three feet long and had been thrown into the water immediately after birth. Several people had observed the remains earlier in the day but thought it was a dead animal. Upon closer inspection, they were horrified to discover it was a human body.

One of the saddest of these unsolved cases occurred on February 9, 1908. A woman crossing the Superior Avenue Viaduct in Cleveland was observed carrying a new suitcase. While standing above the railroad tracks on the east bank, she dropped the suitcase over the side and hurried away. Patrick McCraith, the gateman at the Big Four Railroad crossing below the viaduct, discovered the suitcase lying on the tracks. When he opened it, he discovered the broken body of a six-day-old female child. The coroner investigated the case and determined that the child was alive when it was thrown from the viaduct. The identities of the child and mother remain unknown. The site of this tragedy is now the intersection of West Superior Avenue and Robert Lockwood Jr. Drive on the east bank of the flats.

There are at least four solved cases in Northern Ohio that involve the use of a bridge in disposing of a child. On Sunday, March 6, 1842, the body of an infant child was discovered floating in the Ohio and Erie Canal, under the old Market Street Bridge, between Locks 8 and 9 in Akron. A coroner's inquest was held, and it was determined that the child was murdered by its mother, Emaline Clink. The body was found with two cords tied tightly about its neck. Emaline Clink, who had only been married for a few months, claimed that the child was stillborn, and the reason for her disposing of the remains was to hide the birth from her husband. She never explained why she'd tied cords around its neck.

On June 21, 1858, as two boys were playing near the river just above the old wire bridge in Tiffin, the body of an infant was discovered on the bank with a stone tied around its neck. Realizing what they'd found, the boys became frightened, returned the remains to the river and ran home. After

East end of the Superior Viaduct in Cleveland in 1910, where a six-day-old child was killed two years earlier. *Courtesy Cleveland Public Library Photograph Collection.*

they reported their find, a party assembled and went back to the river, but the light was failing and the search suspended. The next morning, the body was recovered, and an inquest was held, after which the remains were properly interred. It was determined that the child's mother, a young woman by the name of Gardner living in Fort Ball, had been the victim of adultery. There were conflicting reports about whether or not the child was alive when it was put in the river.

Another tragic tale occurred in Cleveland in 1883. On June 10, a twenty-one-year-old German immigrant named Lizzie Schacht gave birth to a little boy out of wedlock. According to Schacht, the child was stillborn. The next day, she placed the lifeless body into a satchel belonging to Carolina Fuchs, with whom she lived. The following day, she tossed the satchel into the river from the Big Four Railroad Bridge. Four days later, the satchel and its contents were found in the river near the Columbus Street Bridge. Lizzie Schacht was identified as the mother and was arrested for murder on June 20, 1883.

At first, Schacht denied being the child's mother, but after Fuchs identified the satchel as belonging to her and two witnesses recognized Schacht as being on the bridge with the satchel, she broke down in tears. Dr. Holliday performed the postmortem on the remains but, due to advanced decomposition, was unable to determine if the child was born alive. The most damning evidence against Schacht was a strip of linen tied around the child's neck. Lizzie Schacht explained that she was afraid the child might start breathing. She was initially found guilty of strangling the child and dumping it into the Cuyahoga River.

A rehearing occurred on July 12 before Judge Tilden, who declared Lizzie Schacht innocent of the charge of infanticide. She maintained that the child was stillborn and was only carried to seven months. She went on to state that the child was born in the morning and that the piece of cloth was tied around its neck later that day. Judge Tilden declared that he believed Schacht's statements to be true and ruled her innocent. Prosecutor Stone fully agreed with the verdict, and the girl was released.

The last story occurred on June 13, 1939, when eleven-week-old Haldon Baker Fink was reported abducted from his crib at his mother's home near Clyde. A search began, and about twelve hours later, his lifeless body was discovered in Green Creek near the U.S. 20 bridge near Fremont. The story drew much media attention, and later that week, a lie detector was brought in. It was learned late that Saturday night that the child's mother, Velma Fink, had taken the child and thrown him into the creek while still alive. Her

The railroad bridge in the Cleveland Flats where Lizzie Schacht threw her child into the river. *Courtesy Cleveland Public Library Photograph Collection.*

reason for this was that she and her husband had divorced a week earlier, and she'd argued with her mother over the future care of the child. She was immediately arrested and charged with murder, to which she entered a plea of not guilty on the basis of temporary insanity.

Her trial began on September 12 and continued for a little less than two weeks. A jury of four men and eight women found her not guilty by reason of temporary insanity. She was remanded to the State Hospital for the Criminally Insane at Lima on September 25 and remained there until November 15, at which time she was released into the care of her family physician, having shown no signs of insanity since entering the institution.

It should be noted that none of the bridges mentioned in this section—all locations where true cases of infanticide are known to have occurred—have ever been noted for producing supernatural sounds of children crying.

CHAPTER V

HAUNTED TAVERNS AND LODGINGS

INTRODUCTION

Haunted houses are widespread throughout Northern Ohio. Haunted taverns and lodgings, on the other hand, are something of a rarity. Some hold historic significance due to the fact that they also served as stops on the Underground Railroad. Fortunately, nearly all of these locations are open to the public or will be in the near future.

WOLF CREEK TAVERN

Located on the southeast corner of State Route 261 and Cleveland-Massillon Road in Norton is the historic Wolf Creek Tavern. This famous restaurant and watering hole, which has a sign out front that states that it was established in 1840, has a noted haunted reputation that goes back many years.

There are at least two specters said to haunt the site. One of these is a woman who, it is believed, dates from when the place was a speakeasy. The other is said to be a man named Ray Wilhelm, who, stories claim, hanged himself in 1886 following a rejection from a lady. Legends also say that Ray is buried in the cemetery behind the tavern and that his ghost haunts the barroom.

An oral history of Wolf Creek Tavern claims that it served as a store, bar, hotel, hospital, prison, brothel, speakeasy, fire station and restaurant. Interestingly, factual history tends to differ from what we've heard or what's been passed along from owner to owner.

In order to understand the legends, it's best to look at the entire history of the place. The history of Wolf Creek Tavern begins with Jacob and Rachel Brown of Waterford, Virginia. They married in January 1807, and their first child, Thomas, was born later that year. The Browns moved to Akron in the spring of 1827, and Jacob became a justice of the peace and opened the first brick combination hotel and store, May's Block.

On August 12, 1830, Jacob and Rachel Brown purchased eighty-seven acres on the southeast corner of Bates' Corners, which was the original name of the village of Loyal Oak, where Wolf Creek Tavern now stands. That same year, Thomas Brown relocated from Akron and built the first store at Bates' Corners upon his parents' property at the crossroads. This was a simple two-story wooden structure with a flat roof. That part of the building still exists and is now the kitchen for the restaurant and the room above it. This newly discovered information places a construction date of the building in 1830—ten years earlier than previously believed.

Upon moving to Bates' Corners, Thomas Brown met a young widow named Elizabeth Bates. Her first husband, Talcott Bates, had died three years earlier. Thomas Brown and the widow Bates were married in 1831.

In 1834, Thomas purchased from his parents the little quarter-acre lot upon which he'd built his store. That fall, he purchased a lot at Norton Center on the southwest corner of the Public Square. There, he began to build another structure that would become a house and store. Upon making that second purchase, he moved with his wife and their children to Norton Center and rented out the store at Bates' Corners. Thomas Brown never saw the completion of the new store at Norton Center; he died within a year of the family's relocation.

For the next fifteen years, Elizabeth Brown continued to live at Norton Center and rented out the old store at Bates' Corners. In 1851, she sold it to George Reimer and moved to Michigan. It's not clear how many people occupied Reimer's building, or every use it served, but in 1856, the old stand was occupied by a man named Henry Bechtel, who used it as a cabinet shop.

Between 1865 and 1869, the building was sold four times, ultimately coming into the hands of Peter Lerch and his wife, Lydia, who operated a tavern, hotel and stagecoach stop from the building. At that time, the structure was expanded from a small stand into the building it is today.

The Loyal Oak Hotel, circa 1914. The flat-roofed section at the back of the house is the original 1830 building. *Courtesy Wolf Creek Tavern.*

The same view of the Loyal Oak Hotel as the present-day Wolf Creek Tavern. *Photo by William G. Krejci.*

It's said that Peter Lerch was a heavy drinker. His wife divorced him in 1876 as a result of his habitual drunkenness. To make matters worse, Peter Lerch was infirm and had difficulty running the business on his own. After his wife left him, he brought on Robert Knecht to operate the hotel. Knecht, whose family operated a cider mill up the road, made a few enemies in 1881, when he testified in court against a neighbor named Deible.

In the early morning hours of the day following that trial, Deible, along with two other men, sought out Knecht at the Loyal Oak House, as the place was then called. The men requested breakfast and to speak with Knecht. When Knecht came down the stairs some minutes later, Deible heaved a large lead weight, which struck Knecht in the shoulder and put a hole in the wall. Had it hit him in the head, it surely would've killed him. The two brawled on the floor. Knecht got the better of Deible, who fled but was found the next day and arrested for assault.

In October 1883, Dr. Austin T. Woods, a local physician, moved his office into the east room of the Loyal Oak House, where he remained until 1901.

During the summer of 1886, management of the Loyal Oak House was taken over by the Wilhelm family. Hiram Wilhelm and his wife, Jessie, moved into the house with their children Ray, Susie, Charles and Mattie. Their eldest child, Ray Crawford Wilhelm, was born on May 24, 1870. Ray wasn't short for Raymond—it was his mother's maiden name.

On Wednesday, August 26, 1886, Ray Wilhelm became a bartender at the Loyal Oak House. To mark the occasion, he signed and dated his name on a wall in an upstairs room. In later years, this would give rise to the legend of a bartender named Ray Wilhelm being rejected by a lady and taking his own life by hanging himself in the hotel. It should be noted that Ray Wilhelm didn't kill himself that day, but for a time after, he did live a troubled life.

On July 17, 1894, Ray robbed a man named Judson B. Merwin of seventy-five dollars, a diamond and a gold watch and chain. He had delivered a message to Merwin earlier that day from a woman named Clara Gretz requesting him to call on her that evening. The next morning, Merwin reported the items missing. Ray was the prime suspect and admitted to the theft but claimed that Clara Gretz was an accomplice. After nothing incriminating was found in her possession, charges against her were dropped. Ray Wilhelm was sentenced to one year in the state penitentiary.

After being released, Ray Wilhelm enlisted with the army and served in the Philippines during the Spanish-American War. He returned a few years later, moved to Cleveland, married and died there on October 30,

1948. He's buried at Whitehaven Cemetery in Mayfield Heights, not in the cemetery at Loyal Oak, as stories claim.

Peter Lerch, however, is buried in the cemetery at Loyal Oak. He died in 1900 and was laid to rest beside his first wife, who died in 1852. The year after Peter Lerch's death, two men named Sulzbach and Yeneyen rented the hotel. Peter Lerch's surviving widow sold the tavern in 1903 to John McNamara, who rented it out to a woman named Ellenore Goodwin. In 1912, George W. Sloat purchased the tavern from McNamara.

On June 28, 1920, Adam and Anna Pinter, with Martin and Rose Nieder, purchased the tavern. The nation had just gone dry, but that didn't stop Pinter. He attempted to continue to sell alcohol at the Loyal Oak Tavern but was arrested by Sheriff Pat Hutchinson on June 24, 1921, for violating Prohibition laws by selling beer containing 4.4 percent alcohol. Afterward, Pinter installed the speakeasy in the basement. He operated the business as Adam's Place, dubbing it a lunch hall, but after Prohibition ended, it became Adam's Inn and reverted back to a tavern. The place also housed the fire department in a barn on the property.

After serving for many years as the Loyal Oak Tavern, the place was purchased by its current owners, Shane and Amy Moore, and reopened as the Wolf Creek Tavern in May 2014.

Something that is widely overlooked is the fact that the building was once a stop on the Underground Railroad. This shouldn't be the least bit surprising. The Browns, who built the first structure on the site, were Quakers, a group highly noted as being active in the abolitionist movement. A tunnel once existed on the site that ran from the northeast corner of the basement (which was in the original section of the building), under the road and to a building that once stood across the street on the northeast corner of the intersection.

The ghostly lady, whomever she is, has been seen multiple times by many people near the oldest section of the building at the top of the stairs.

WEST RICHFIELD HOTEL

Located at 3960 Broadview Road in Richfield is a stately old tavern and hotel that boasts many amenities. Of interest is the large barroom and double dining room on the first floor, a second-floor ballroom, a subterranean saloon—and ghosts aplenty.

According to legend, the building is primarily haunted by its original owner, a man named Baxter Wood, who built the place in the 1880s. He appears as a tall, bearded man in a black suit and top hat, standing in the barroom. Others have reported seeing his ghostly figure standing at the top of the stairs to the second floor. In recent years, two more spirits have joined the cast. This occurred following the installation of a stained-glass window bearing the name Rebecca Aker. It's said that the ghosts of Rebecca and her son Elijah followed the window to its current location in the 1990s after the window's original home, a church near Dayton, was gutted by a fire.

Aside from its beautifully appointed facilities, the building also features a colorful and historic past in which legend has been blurred with facts. The truth of the matter is as follows.

Baxter Henry Wood was born in Holland, Massachusetts, on February 19, 1827. In 1838, he traveled with his family to Ohio and settled in West Richfield. Six years later, he entered the mercantile business with his father and brother and operated a store in a building that was located on the northwest corner of what are now State Routes 176 and 303. In 1864, Wood relocated to Medina County and entered the lumber trade. His younger brother Charles continued the firm with a new partner named Henry C. Searles. That partnership lasted for ten years.

Around that time, the old corner where the store was located was redeveloped into a triangular park, and a new street called Ellsworth Avenue was installed along the western edge. The buildings located in the new park were torn down, and the construction of buildings along the new street to the west was soon underway. One of these new buildings became the home of the mercantile firm of Searles and Wood.

When Charles Wood dissolved his partnership with Henry Searles around 1874, he briefly remained on the site before opening a new mercantile on the south side of State Route 303. Searles moved back into the store on the triangle and opened a merchandising firm with a man named Phillips. On October 2, 1876, that store burned but was rebuilt within the year. It was completely destroyed by a second fire on October 8, 1885.

Although he resided in Medina County, Baxter Henry Wood ended up purchasing the lot that had been occupied by those two previous stores, and in 1886, he began construction on a new hotel and stagecoach stop. He named the new business the West Richfield Hotel.

According to the book *Fifty Years and Over of Akron and Summit County*, which was written in 1892, the West Richfield Hotel was

The West Richfield Hotel, circa 1890. *Courtesy Richfield Historical Society.*

a new and well-appointed hotel on the site of the store formerly occupied by ex-recorder Henry C. Searles, near the northwest corner of the Public Square, owned by Mr. Baxter H. Wood of Medina, but kept by Richfield's veteran landlord Lewis P. Ellas.

This suggests that Baxter Wood owned the hotel but didn't live in or operate it. That honor fell upon Lewis Ellas.

Lewis Primrose Ellas was born in May 1834 in Tioga County, New York. In 1860, he was living in Bath, Summit County, where he kept a tavern. Soon after, he relocated to Richfield and kept a hotel there through the early 1880s.

It would also appear that Baxter Henry Wood only owned the hotel for a few short years. By the early 1890s, it was owned by a real estate broker named Ferdinand J. Creque, who continued to rent to Ellas.

Ellas died in March 1902 and was buried in West Richfield Cemetery. Shortly before his passing, operation of the hotel was taken over by the Carter family, and the business was briefly called the Carter House. Within a few years, the name reverted back to the West Richfield Hotel. Other operators of the hotel were the Viall, Chaffee and Hotz families.

During the Prohibition years, the building was run as a barbershop under the proprietorship of Michael and Julia Gyenge. Claims have been made that Michael Gyenge operated a speakeasy through that period. By 1940, the building was again being used as a beer parlor.

Michael Gyenge passed away in 1944. Later that year, operation was taken over by Joseph Smee, who reopened it as the Underground Tavern. It continued under that name until shortly before Smee's death in 1970. For the next few years, the building sat empty.

In 1977, the old hotel was extensively remodeled by its new owner, Mel Rose, and opened near the end of that year as the Taverne of Richfield. It's been suggested that Rose's ownership was the most lucrative the place had known. The Richfield Coliseum was located nearby, and many people would stop in for dinner before sporting events.

The Coliseum closed in 1994, and two years later, so did the Taverne of Richfield. From 1998 to 2006, the building housed Stancato's Cafe. After it changed hands again, the name Taverne of Richfield was resurrected.

In February 2018, the Taverne of Richfield closed. Later that year, it was announced that the building would become the new home of Olesia's Place. The old hotel underwent another major restoration prior to opening.

Stories of the old West Richfield Hotel claim that Baxter Wood's ghost haunts the place. Why he would haunt a building that he briefly owned and never lived in is anyone's guess. Of course, it's impossible to know exactly who haunts any given location, but it should be noted that the ghost described in the story very much resembles a photo of Lewis Ellas that once hung in the old tavern.

As it turns out, the stained-glass windows weren't from Dayton. They came from the old Mulberry Street United Methodist Church, located in Mt. Vernon, which was being demolished in 1977. Nearly every window bears a name. Rebecca Aker is just one of many.

Rebecca Aker was born in 1821 as Rebecca Cassell. She married Elisha Bowman Aker and resided in Fredericktown, a few miles north of Mt. Vernon. She and her husband had two children, Ann and Mary. Where the idea of the Akers having a son named Elijah originated remains a mystery.

PUNDERSON MANOR

Nestled on the banks of Punderson Lake, just west of Burton in Geauga County, is Punderson Manor. This striking Tudor-style building claims stories of ghostly encounters, including doors slamming, various items being tossed about and the sounds of children laughing when none are present. Some have suggested that the source of the haunting lies in the old manor's past.

Ten years after Moses Cleaveland brought his first survey party into the Western Reserve and established the city of Cleveland in 1796, another man from Connecticut named Lemuel Punderson arrived and established a mill and distillery on the south end of a glacial lake called the Big Pond. Punderson died suddenly in 1822. Following his death, his family remained in the area and continued to make a living off the land. Eventually, the name of the pond was changed to Punderson Lake to honor the early settler.

In 1902, a man named William Bingham Cleveland purchased the land surrounding the lake. Two years later, he built a large house on the property, which he called Lakefield Farm and Kennel. On that site, he bred dogs and kept all manner of animals, including wolves, goats and bison. During the early 1920s, Cleveland developed cancer and found that he could no longer handle the day-to-day operations of the farm. Management was taken over by Dr. Everette Peter Coppedge, the brother of his wife, Ocie. A few years later, Lakefield Farm was sold to a man named Karl Everette Long. William Cleveland passed away on July 20, 1929, at his home in Cleveland Heights.

It's been said that William Cleveland was a direct descendant of Moses Cleaveland. While he does have an ancestor named Moses, he was not the same man who founded Cleveland, Ohio.

The new owner of the Punderson Lake property, Karl Long, was the owner of Long Transportation Company, a trucking firm that shipped automobiles. He was an Ohio native but spent much of his adulthood residing in Detroit. Shortly after purchasing Lakefield Farm, he planned to build a new home on the property. The Cleveland family hoped that he would simply modify the existing home on the site, but Long demolished it, saving only a couple of chimneys. On the former site of the home, he commenced construction of a Tudor-style home.

It's been suggested that Karl Long lost his fortune following the stock market crash of 1929 and, as a result, defaulted on the Punderson Lake property. It's also claimed that he committed suicide by hanging himself in the attic of his half-finished home on the lake. In truth, Long didn't lose his fortune, nor did he take his own life. He died at his home in Detroit on December 6, 1932, at the age of forty-six. His cause of death was cerebral apoplexy brought on by hypertension.

Following his death, the Punderson Lake property returned to the hands of the Cleveland family, who still owned the title on the mortgage. In 1932,

A snowy day at Punderson Manor. *Photo by William G. Krejci.*

Ocie Brown Cleveland, William Cleveland's widow, remarried and moved back to her hometown of Stanton, Tennessee. The farm became Lakefield Camp during the late 1930s and early 1940s. All 505 acres were sold to the State of Ohio in 1948 and became Punderson State Park, which opened in 1951. The beautiful house that Karl Long was building on the site was finished by the state and became Punderson Manor, which now serves as a lodge, resort and conference center.

In regard to the haunting of Punderson Manor, legends claim that a summer resort called the Wales Hotel once stood across the lake. In 1885, there was a fire in the hotel, and many children were killed. It's believed that these are the children who now haunt the manor.

The truth of the matter is that James E. Wales didn't begin construction on the Wales Hotel until late 1888. It opened the following spring, four years after this devastating fire is supposed to have happened. Wales died in 1919, and the hotel closed in March 1925. It was torn down by William Cleveland shortly after it closed.

Another story that attempts to explain the ghostly events says that the manor is haunted by people who drowned on Punderson Lake. Sadly, there have been many drownings on the lake. Some of these occurred in recent years and won't be mentioned, as it's sure to be a sensitive subject for surviving family members.

One that will be mentioned is the sad case of twenty-one-year-old Robert Julius Neubauer of Warrensville. On July 15, 1904, he and a friend named

Archibald Gates went to Punderson Lake to spend a quiet afternoon. They rented a boat and rowed to the middle of the lake. Thinking that the boat would remain in place, they jumped in and went for a swim. After a few minutes, they realized that the boat had been blown by the wind and drifted away. Neubauer swam for the boat but was unable to reach it before being overcome with exhaustion. He sank just ten feet away from the boat and never resurfaced.

Over the course of the next few days, attempts were made to recover the body, but the search was eventually called off. The bottom of Punderson Lake is composed of quicksand in places, and it's believed that Neubauer's body may have ended up in such an area. Punderson Lake remains his burial site to this day.

A curious event transpired at Punderson State Park in early October 1990. At that time, a massive search was made on the grounds for a buried body or bodies. A tip had come in from a woman from New York who claimed that a murderer had buried someone at the site many years earlier. The search went on for four days but was called off after nothing was found. Interestingly, a murder mystery fitting the exact same scenario that the woman described had been performed the previous October at Punderson Manor. The identity of the tipster was never made public, nor were the circumstances of her claim.

So, who haunts Punderson Manor? Certainly not children who died in a fictional hotel fire or a business owner from Detroit who never hanged himself in the attic.

OLD STONE HOUSE BED AND BREAKFAST

Located just south of the crossroads at Mesopotamia, at 8505 State Route 534, is the Old Stone House Bed and Breakfast. Though it was not known by this name at the time, it made the news twice in 1900.

In November of that year, a story in the *Cleveland Plain Dealer* stated that the old house was once again occupied after more than twenty-five years of dereliction. Thirty years earlier, a family of good means had occupied the house. The parents died, and their two sons continued to reside there. When one of the sons passed, his grief-stricken brother left the house, vowing never to return. All of the furnishings, pantry provisions and even the owner's clothes were left in a perfect state of abandonment. The article concluded by saying that the new owners had taken over the property and returned it to a habitable state.

A little over a month later, the *Plain Dealer* ran another article with the headline "A Tale of a Haunted Ohio House." The article told a similar story but gave names and particulars of those involved. It referred to the house as the Old Ford Place and claimed that it was last occupied by John and Jerry Ford. The two brothers occupied the house after the deaths of their parents and continued to operate the farm. These two bachelors only had each other, and when John died, Jerry abandoned the house, leaving everything just as it was on the day of John's passing.

The twist in the story came when it was claimed that one of Jerry's nieces asked for permission to see the house. He had no objections, and she went to the old place with her mother. By that point, the home had been abandoned for nearly twenty-five years and had gained the reputation of being a haunted house. No one dared to go anywhere near it.

The two women braved the ghostly legends and entered the house, finding it in decay. Among the many forsaken items in the house, they found crumbling legal papers and, in an old compartment chest, $500 in gold and silver coins. Today, these would carry a value of nearly $14,000.

They reported their find to Jerry, who was uninterested. A few weeks later, the women returned to recover the treasure but found that someone else had broken in and stolen the coins. Jerry Ford passed away shortly after, and as was stated in the *Plain Dealer* article, new tenants had restored the house.

As is so often the case, fact and fiction intertwine, and before long, a legend is born. The true story is that the stately house was built around 1825 by Colonel Jesse Pinney Holcomb. Colonel Holcomb was the son of Revolutionary War veteran Captain Jesse Holcomb and his wife, Louisa Pinney. Jesse's grandfather Hezekiah Holcomb was the original property owner. Colonel Jesse Holcomb lived in the house until 1830. At that time, Mark Ford was living on the western edge of Mesopotamia Township. He and his brother-in-law Job Reynolds owned a number of lots in that area. In 1830, Ford traded one of those lots, consisting of two hundred acres, with the one near town that contained the stone house.

Mark Ford died in June 1850 and was laid to rest at Fairview Cemetery in Mesopotamia. The house continued to be occupied by his widow, Aylsey, and sons Hiram, George and Freeman. Aylsey Ford died in 1863, and the house and farm entered the possession of Hiram Ford. His younger brother George continued to reside with him, while Freeman and his wife moved

Old Stone House Bed and Breakfast in Mesopotamia, the scene of a historic haunting. *Photo by William G. Krejci.*

to another home. Incidentally, Hiram and George are the real names of the brothers whom the newspaper article misidentified as John and Jerry Ford, respectively. Hiram died in 1871, at which time George abandoned the house and moved in with his brother Freeman.

The article states that a niece and her mother visited the deserted house. In truth, George had no nieces. This was likely his nephew Jesse's wife, Grace, and her mother, Julia Brigden.

George Ford died in 1896, and the farm was divided between his two nephews. Elsworth Ford got the majority of the land, while Jesse received the house. Jesse and Grace were the people who restored it. The house changed hands a few times over the next century and now operates as the Old Stone House Bed and Breakfast.

But is it haunted? Some would say no and suspect that the newspaper article from 1900 was just sensationalism. According to Darcy Miller, who has owned the Old Stone House since 1984, this is not the case. Originally, the house was rather quiet, but it went through a very noisy period for some time after Miller moved in. Unexplained noises are still heard throughout the house from time to time. What's more, many visitors have witnessed the apparition of a young boy in the home. Occasionally, paranormal investigators have stayed the night and recorded EVP (electronic voice phenomena) and captured photographic anomalies.

Aside from this, the house has also drawn numerous treasure hunters who believe that the Ford brothers buried their fortune on the property. Not surprisingly, the "treasure" hasn't been found. Perhaps that's because the Ford brothers never buried their money—as previously stated, it was kept in an old compartment chest in the house.

RIDER'S INN

Painesville's celebrated Rider's Inn, located at 792 Mentor Avenue, is a true Lake County treasure. It is home to a bed and breakfast, restaurant, pub and a haunted history centered around three ghosts.

Joseph Rider was born on September 3, 1771, in Willington, Connecticut. In 1803, he traveled west to Ohio with his wife, Phoebe, and their children. The Rider family first settled in Fairport Harbor, where Joseph built a log cabin. Three years later, Phoebe Rider passed away.

In 1808, Joseph married again. His new wife was named Roxany Gaylord. Within two years, he'd moved his cabin, logs and all, to the village of Champion, which later became the city of Painesville. The idea of Rider physically relocating the cabin is reinforced by the fact that his son and grandson both worked as building-movers.

In 1818, the log cabin was expanded into a one-story frame structure and began its life as a tavern, inn and stagecoach stop. Around 1822, Painesville's master builder, Jonathan Goldsmith, altered the building and raised it to two stories. This remodeled structure was intended to emulate George Washington's home at Mount Vernon.

Roxany Rider died in 1831, but bachelorhood didn't suit Joseph. He married again on August 30, 1832, to his third wife, Susannah Castle. Unfortunately, the marital bliss was short-lived, as Susannah died within weeks. Again, Joseph Rider sought companionship and married his fourth and final wife, a widow named Mary Wilmot Lockman, on September 24, 1833.

During the mid-1830s, Joseph briefly held a municipal post and served as fence viewer. He did not hold the position for long, as he soon fell ill. Operation of the tavern was handed over to his son Lester. Joseph Rider died on February 22, 1840 and was likely buried in the old Washington Street Cemetery, which is now an empty field in downtown Painesville.

It was during Lester Rider's management in the 1840s that the tavern was first used as a stop on the Underground Railroad. The entrance to one

Rider's Tavern, circa 1900. From a postcard by J.E. Lighter Company. *Courtesy Carl Thomas Engel.*

tunnel was located in a false well to the east of the building. A second tunnel ran to the north and exited at a laundry building by the creek. The ceilings of both of these tunnels were no more than four feet high.

Lester Rider died on August 12, 1847, from consumption. Operation of the tavern was turned over to his younger brother Zerah Rider. Zerah was born in the tavern in 1820 and died there in 1902. Interestingly, he died in the same room where he was born, which was the same room his father had passed away in sixty-two years earlier. After Zerah Rider's death in 1902, the tavern passed to his son, Zerah Perkins Rider. It was then solely used as a private residence and was occupied by Zerah Perkins Rider and his daughter Nellie until 1922.

George A. Randell purchased and remodeled the old tavern in 1923 and reopened it under the name Randell Tavern. During the remodeling, Randell put a one-story addition on the east end of the building. He only had the place for ten years. This was during Prohibition, and it's believed that the addition operated as a speakeasy, as parts of a liquor still were later found hidden away in the back room. Randell went bankrupt in 1933, and the original antique furnishings from the tavern were put up for auction.

In April 1934, Corrine C. Adam and Marie Kalback leased the building from the Cleveland Trust Company and changed the name back to the Rider Tavern. Corinne Adam retired in 1941, and that April, the place was sold to Elizabeth Bassett of Wheaton, Illinois. From 1947 to 1959, it was known as Lutz's Tavern and was operated by brothers Gerald and Park Lutz. From 1960 to 1975, it was called Lutz's Inn. During that time, it was added to the National Register of Historic Places.

On January 9, 1977, the historic tavern was almost lost in a fire. The kitchen and two rooms above it were damaged when a boiler in the kitchen overheated. Damages were estimated at $60,000. At that time, it was owned by Frank Carroll, who had bought it in 1969 and had recently changed the name back to Rider's Inn. It changed hands again in 1979, when Daniel McLeod purchased and renovated the structure. In 1988, it was purchased and restored by Elaine Crane, who continues to operate it today.

In regard to the haunting of Rider's Inn, it's said that at least three entities have been witnessed in the building. The first is said to be a man dressed in a Civil War uniform. His identity is something of a mystery. The other two ghosts are believed to be Joseph Rider's second and third wives, Roxany and Susannah. It's said that Roxany is a fairly helpful spirit. Susannah, on the other hand, seems to be a bit more mischievous. On more than one occasion, Elaine Crane has discovered people either coming up the stairs after hours or in an upstairs bedroom the next morning. They told the same story each time—they all claimed that they'd been let in by a woman in a white nightgown. When the door was checked, it was locked.

In time, Rider's Inn was visited by a woman named Elizabeth Brainard, a descendant of Joseph Rider. Through Brainard, it was learned that the front door being opened by the mystery woman was not a new thing. She explained that it was Susannah Rider's ghost showing her hospitality. Originally, it was the old front door in the tavern room that Susannah opened. The Riders eventually had to seal the door to stop her from doing this. It's said that it took nearly two hundred nails to effectively complete the task. It was after that tavern room door was nailed shut that Susannah moved to the front door. Despite the front door occasionally being mysteriously opened, the current owner has no plans to nail it shut.

Unionville Tavern

A historical marker outside the old tavern at 7935 South Ridge Road in Madison Township in Lake County states that it was built as the Webster House. It was later known as the New England House and, more recently, as the Old Tavern. The marker further states that it was constructed from two cabins in 1798. In the years leading up to the Civil War, it served as a stop on the Underground Railroad. It's a fantastic story, but with the exception of the tavern serving as an Underground Railroad stop, hardly any of it is true.

While the building is composed of two log structures, the first of these wasn't built until 1805. That first cabin can be attributed to a man named Blanchard.

Ira Devestus Blanchard was born in Stamford, Connecticut, on July 14, 1785. As a young man, he traveled to Ohio and built a log tavern at the crossroads of the South Ridge and County Line Roads in Unionville. In 1806, Blanchard married Lydia Mills Case. Sadly, their marriage was brief, as Ira died in July 1808.

Two months after Ira's death, Lydia gave birth to a son, whom she named Ira. Just over a month later, Lydia joined her husband in death. The infant Ira Blanchard was raised by Lydia's brother Asahel Case in Oberlin. Interestingly, Ira Blanchard Jr. became a doctor and a well-known abolitionist in Iowa. He was a conductor on the Underground Railroad, with his house being one of the first stops runaway slaves came to in the free territory. He'd been born in the old tavern, so it seemed fitting that his birthplace would become an iconic stop on the Underground Railroad.

Within a few years of the deaths of Ira and Lydia Blanchard, the log tavern was rented out to the Mixer family.

Phineas Mixer was born in 1756 in Dudley, Massachusetts. He and his wife, Abigail, along with their children, arrived in Madison Township on January 24, 1805. In early 1811, Phineas Mixer relocated to Unionville and took up residency at the former Blanchard tavern. Mixer continued to rent the tavern until 1817, at which time he purchased it and the adjoining ninety-three-acre farm. He built a second log structure, connected to the first, on the site and operated a post office.

Phineas Mixer died in 1821. His children continued to operate the farm, but the tavern was taken over by his son Julius Usebus Mixer.

Of particular note is an event known as the County Line Road Incident. During the summer of 1843, two fugitive slaves named Milton and Lewis Clarke, who had been residing in Oberlin, came to speak at an antislavery rally in Unionville. Milton Clarke was beaten and captured by bounty hunters but was released when the people of Unionville freed him. Afterward, it was vowed by the people of Unionville that no runaway slave would ever be taken by bounty hunters in that town. Some years later, Harriet Beecher Stowe stayed at the Unionville Tavern and heard the story of the Clarke brothers. It's been suggested that Milton Clarke inspired the character of George Harris in Stowe's 1852 novel *Uncle Tom's Cabin*.

As the late 1840s approached, Julius Mixer sought to retire from keeping the tavern. He found a new owner, a man named Shears.

Spencer Shears, Esq. (or "Spence," as he preferred), took over the stand in Unionville in September 1849. Previously, he'd operated the Franklin House in Ashtabula. Upon taking possession of the tavern, he repainted and rearranged the entire building and renamed it the New England House. It was said that Spencer Shears was

> *a host of himself, the very prince of good fellows. Entertainment for man and beast seemed to stick-out from his good-natured phiz all over.*

The Shears family enjoyed a time of prosperity while running the tavern. Of course, they kept up the tradition of harboring fugitive slaves. Many dances were held in the second-floor ballroom, while those who were on the run were safely secreted in the tunnels beneath the large tavern. Spencer Shears also served as Unionville's postmaster.

Things were pretty uneventful in Unionville until 1855. On the evening of June 13, the tavern received a guest who took a room for the night. He never gave a name, nor did he sign a registry. He simply went to his room and slept. After breakfast the following morning, the guest came out of his room and took a seat behind the stove. He'd been the picture of good health the night before, but he now began to sigh and breathe heavily and ultimately laid his head on the side of the stove. When he made no answer to inquiries regarding his health from those around him, someone lifted his head and found him to be dead.

Unionville Tavern, from a postcard dated 1908. *Courtesy Carl Thomas Engel.*

There were only a few items in his possession that could give a clue to his identity. He had in his room a carpetbag, which contained two pairs of spectacles, a tin cup, a plug of tobacco, a knife, some clothes, two dollars and fifty cents in cash, a pencil and a copy of *Phelps' Traveling Guide* with a name and address written in pencil, "T. E. Courtney, North-west corner of Main and Olive Street – H. 3 & Olive."

The justice of the peace held an inquest concerning the body, and it was determined that the mysterious visitor was somewhere around the age of fifty, showed no marks of violence and "came to his death in a way and manner unknown to the jury—probably by the visitation of God." The remains were respectfully buried in the village cemetery.

In January 1859, Spencer Shears fell ill and handed over the postmaster duties to Daniel Cleveland. Shears died on May 24, 1859, and was buried in Alexander Harper Memorial Cemetery in Unionville. His widow, Minerva, continued to operate the tavern for the next few years before turning over operations to William A. Webster. He renamed the tavern the Webster House. Minerva continued to own the tavern until 1866, when she sold it to Clark Martin.

In June 1885, the tavern changed hands again and became Taylor's Hotel under the ownership of Robinson Taylor. The accommodation boasted of pure air and healthy water, with mineral springs located nearby. It was also stated that the hotel never had any fever or malaria, which must have come as a relief to visitors. After Robinson Taylor's death, Taylor's Hotel was run by his widow, Harriet.

By 1910, the hotel had closed and was listed on maps simply as the "Old Tavern." After an extensive restoration, it was reopened in the 1920s by Arthur E. Fritz and his wife, Hulda. By the 1940s, the business was operating under the name Ye Olde Tavern.

Ghost stories claim that the spirit of a runaway slave haunts the old tavern, grounds and tunnels under the building. These tunnels were said to lead into the old graveyard, located diagonally across the street, where they terminated at a false grave. In actuality, the tunnel that ran toward the cemetery terminated on the corner of the cemetery lot, where a store owned by postmaster Daniel Cleveland stood.

Why the specter of a runaway slave would haunt the Unionville Tavern is anyone's guess. It seems more likely that the place would be haunted by someone who actually lived or died there, such as any one of the people who owned it over the last two centuries. There's also the case of the mysterious visitor who suddenly died in 1855. Nothing more was known of the man—until now.

After conducting extensive research for this book, I managed to discover that "T. E. Courtney, North-west corner of Main and Olive Street" was none other than Thomas Edgeworth Courtenay of St. Louis, Missouri. The name had been misspelled in the newspaper. Courtenay, who had southern ties though his wife's family, kept an insurance office at that address during the mid-1850s. It should be noted that the mysterious visitor who died in Unionville was *not* Thomas Courtenay, who, it's well-documented, remained in the insurance business until January 1860, at which time he was appointed sheriff of St. Louis County, replacing the previous sheriff, who had recently died. That August, Courtenay's term was over, and he relocated to Maryland with his family.

Here's where things get interesting.

During the Civil War, Thomas E. Courtenay sided with the Confederacy and became a top operative with the Confederate Secret Service. He was also the inventor of the coal torpedo, an explosive device disguised to look like a lump of coal. When shoveled into the stoker of a ship or locomotive, the device would detonate. The coal torpedo is credited with sinking at least two ships, the USS *Greyhound* and the USS *Chenango*.

This still doesn't tell us about the identity of the man that died at Unionville Tavern in 1855. In fact, it only raises more questions. What was a man doing at Spencer Shears's New England House, a known stop on the Underground Railroad, carrying a copy of *Phelps' Traveling Guide* with Thomas Edgeworth Courtenay's name and address on it? Was he a traveling salesman under the employ of Courtenay? This seems unlikely, as most people would purchase insurance from a local agent. Could he have been a bounty hunter searching for runaway slaves? This is possible, as Courtenay's in-laws owned Southern plantations. How did this man really meet his end?

The Unionville Tavern was last open to the public in 2006. Five years later, a movement was started to save the old tavern, and a restoration commenced in early 2017 under the direction of the Unionville Tavern Preservation Society, which now owns the property.

CHAPTER VI

HAUNTED CEMETERIES

INTRODUCTION

As noted in the introduction, simply stating that a place is haunted doesn't necessarily make it so. Cemeteries are no exception to that rule. The ghost stories that follow have been reported by multiple sources and multiple witnesses. Please be respectful when visiting any of these locations and adhere to all posted rules and regulations. Disrespecting burial sites is not in keeping with the spirit of this book.

WOLFINGER CEMETERY

Located in Secor Park just outside of Sylvania in Lucas County is Wolfinger Cemetery. This burial ground was established in August 1835 after the death of seven-year-old Rebecca Louisa Wolfinger, a daughter of Jacob and Margaret Rebecca Harpel Wolfinger, who were the first settlers in that township. Over 180 years later, it is still receiving burials.

The ghost story associated with Wolfinger Cemetery states that it's haunted by three children who died within a couple of weeks of each other. Many have claimed to have witnessed the presence of three ghostly children laughing and playing near the back of the cemetery.

The graves of three children buried at Wolfinger Cemetery. *Photo by William G. Krejci.*

In an older section of the cemetery sits the children's headstone, which only gives their first names, middle initials and dates of birth and death. Thomas, age eight, passed away on December 17, 1865. His twelve-year-old sister, Rebecca, died five days later. Earnest, who was only six, died on January 2, 1866. Interestingly, no surname appears on the stone, so their identity has remained a mystery—until now.

George Gowman was born in Hampshire, England, in 1823. He arrived in the United States with his family in the mid-1830s and settled in Cleveland. By 1850, the Gowmans were living in the village of Avon in Lorian County. Within a year, George was married to Ruth Dunton of neighboring Sheffield Township. They became the parents of six children.

George enlisted with Company A of the 128th Ohio Infantry Regiment on August 15, 1864. At this, Ruth took their children and moved in with the family of George's brother Thomas, who lived on North Berkey Southern Road in Richfield Township, Lucas County. George was stationed as a guard at the Confederate prison on Johnson's Island. When his company mustered out on June 9, 1865, he went to Lucas County to be with his family. While staying with Thomas's family, three of George and Ruth's children passed away and were buried at Wolfinger Cemetery. Family records confirm this.

By 1870, the Gowmans were living in Elyria, where George operated a saloon. Ruth passed away in August 1888. George followed in 1896 and is buried beside her at Ridgelawn Cemetery in Elyria, where two more of their children are also buried.

RIVER STYX CEMETERY

In 1816, brothers John and David Wilson arrived in Guilford Township, Medina County, and began clearing land for a community they would call Wilson's Corners. To avoid confusion with another place with that name, the name was ultimately changed to River Styx. This curious name was taken from the nearby river. According to John's son Tom Wilson, the Native Americans had already called it that, possibly because of the vast number of logs that washed up along the banks every spring. He also surmised that a swampy area to the south of the settlement may have lent some influence to the naming of the river, with the wetland in question being impossible to navigate.

Two years after arriving, David Wilson married Abigail Porter. November 1821 saw the passing of Elijah Porter, Abigail's grandfather, who was a Revolutionary War veteran and a hero of the Battle of Bunker Hill. Elijah Porter had set out for Medina to deal with business related to his war pension.

In 1844, David Wilson built this vault at River Styx Cemetery to deter grave robbers. *Photo by William G. Krejci.*

He'd borrowed a horse from David Wilson to make the trip, but that evening, the horse returned without its rider. A search was made, and Elijah Porter was found gravely wounded, lying beside a tree. He had severely lacerated his leg by snagging it on a branch. The wound being too great, Elijah Porter died from massive blood loss and was buried on land belonging to David Wilson. Thus, River Styx Cemetery was established.

Throughout its early years, there was a problem of frequent grave-robbing at the cemetery. Resurrectionists were all too often unearthing fresh burials and selling the bodies to a medical school in nearby Wadsworth. In 1844, David Wilson took matters into his own hands and erected a cemetery vault. *A History of Medina County*, from 1881, describes the vault:

> *At Wilson's Corners, there having been several cases of grave-robbing, the citizens constructed quite a large receiving vault in their little cemetery a short distance south from the village. This vault is still in good condition, and is the only one of the kind in Guilford Township.*

The vault was built into the side of the hill and held coffins long enough for decay to take hold on the bodies, making them undesirable for use as medical cadavers. Originally, the vault was sealed with a large wooden door, but grave robbers were still occasionally able to get in. One story states that David Wilson's wife's body was even pilfered from the vault. According to the story, he tracked down the culprits and reclaimed her remains at gunpoint. In 1894, the wooden door was replaced with an iron gate that was made by blacksmith William A. Krout.

Concerning the haunting of River Styx Cemetery, people claim to witness restless apparitions in and around the empty hillside vault.

CHOLERA CEMETERY

Originally opened as the Harrison Street Cemetery, Cholera Cemetery was Sandusky's second burial ground. The first one is now on the site of Battery Park. The old Harrison Street Cemetery received its first burial on October 23, 1829, with the interment of eighteen-month-old Mary Root, a daughter of Abner and Elizabeth Root. The following February, two infant children of Ogden and Orra Mallory were buried in the small lot. In all, there were more than thirty-six burials in the cemetery between

1829 and 1848. Among these was U.S. congressman William H. Hunter, who died in 1842.

Stories claim that cholera was brought to Sandusky by two people who had fled from Cincinnati on the Mad River Railroad. One of these, a man named Shepard, survived. The other, a German woman, died three days later. Interestingly, no evidence of this exists.

According to newspaper articles from the time, the first death was fifty-two-year-old Sally Allen. She took ill while attending Sunday morning services at the Methodist Episcopal Church on July 1, 1849. Her illness worsened throughout the day, and she passed the following morning at nine o'clock. Sally Allen was the first cholera victim buried at the Harrison Street Cemetery. The emergence of cholera in Sandusky created a panic, and more than 1,500 of its population of 4,000 fled the city to avoid the disease.

For the next two months, nearly four hundred cholera victims followed Sally Allen into that burial ground, with more than sixty people buried in one mass grave in late July. The final interment was the son of Alonzo Edwards, who died on September 11, 1849. His father had died four days earlier.

The cholera abated for some time but returned in 1852 and 1854, though with not as great a death toll as the epidemic of 1849. These later victims were buried at Oakland Cemetery, which opened in 1850.

For the next four decades, Harrison Street Cemetery sat abandoned and neglected. Then, on January 9, 1894, the ground was plowed over and the headstones removed, which angered many residents who still had family members buried there. The site was considered for use as a football field, but residents again protested. Realizing its importance to the people of Sandusky, the site was rededicated as a memorial park on November 16, 1924. A bronze memorial was erected with an inscription at the base that reads:

> *Erected in memory of the pioneers of Sandusky, Ohio, who gave their lives during the cholera epidemic of 1849 to 1854 A.D. During this great tragedy, half of the 4000 population either fled or were called by death. Those remaining rendered worthy service. To their unselfish faithfulness, we owe this tribute of reverence and love.*

An Ohio Historical Society marker placed at the site in 1965 attests to the tragedy that struck the city. The reverse side of the plaque names the doctors who came to aid the citizens of Sandusky.

Originally known as the Harrison Street Cemetery, Cholera Cemetery was rededicated in 1924 and is pictured here in 1925. *Courtesy Sandusky Library Archives Research Center.*

Aside from the memorial and historical society marker, there are also headstones for three veterans of the American Revolution who are said to be buried there. It's uncertain when these were placed, but the stones state that two of the men, John and Joseph Ransom, died in 1840. The third stone is for Robert Ransom, who is believed to have died around 1820.

Interestingly, these are only memorial stones. John and Joseph Ransom, who were cousins, died on October 3, 1840, aboard the schooner *Helen Marr*. They were traveling east when a storm kicked up and sank the schooner off Point Albino, Ontario. Their bodies were never recovered.

An attempt was made to set replacement government headstones for these men in the 1940s, though it appears that the effort was unsuccessful. The application for Robert Ransom's headstone was flatly rejected, as no evidence of him ever existing could be located.

Concerning cholera, a rare but unfortunate symptom of the disease is a coma, which gives a person a death-like appearance. Because cholera is a highly contagious disease, burials were conducted as quickly as possible to prevent further spread of the illness. This, sadly, led to the occasional person being prematurely buried. Cholera Cemetery is said to be haunted by the angry spirits of those who were buried alive.

SHOWMAN–EDWARDS CEMETERY

Deep in the woods of the North Turkeyfoot Wildlife Area of Washington Township in Henry County sits the Showman-Edwards Cemetery. This family burial ground was established on land that originally belonged to David and Cynthia Ann Edwards. The two wed on August 18, 1824, in Clark County and settled on a farm just west of the village of Texas, Ohio. David Edwards served in the War of 1812 as a member of the 1st Regiment of DeLong's Ohio Militia. His father-in-law, John Meek, also a veteran of that war, served as a private in the 2nd Regiment of Hindman's Ohio Militia.

There are at least ten people buried in the Showman-Edwards Cemetery, including David and Cynthia Edwards; Cynthia's father, John; and seven of David and Cynthia's children. One of these children, Sanford Edwards, served as a private in the Civil War with Company C of the Ohio 128th Infantry Regiment.

The name Showman was added to the cemetery in later years as the farm passed into the hands of David and Cynthia's son-in-law Robert W. Showman. It should be noted that no members of the Showman family are buried there.

The vandalized Showman-Edwards Cemetery, where three U.S. veterans take their repose. *Photo by William G. Krejci.*

A visit to the Showman-Edwards Cemetery is a challenge, to say the least. It was once accessible via a small and rickety bridge that has since been removed. The best way to access the site would be to park in the lot just to the west of Turkeyfoot Creek off of Old U.S. Route 24. From there, walk east through the woods until you reach the ruins of a road. To the left are the remnants of the old bridge that crossed the creek. Turn right and walk toward the Maumee River. The cemetery is located on the left. It has largely been destroyed, and the stones have been knocked over and scattered.

The primary ghost story attached to Showman-Edwards Cemetery states that visitors at the site around dusk have witnessed a tall and shadowy human-like figure stalking them through the woods. Another story claims that a man named William Henry Precht died while crossing the old bridge over Turkeyfoot Creek. This second story isn't true. Precht died in 1931 on nearby Old U.S. Route 24 when the tractor he'd hooked up to his beet trailer rolled over and crushed him.

The saddest part of this tale is that the final resting place of two veterans of the War of 1812 and a veteran of the Civil War would be vandalized, disrespected and left in its current condition. It would be nice to see the cemetery restored and these veterans honored with proper memorials.

An Angel at Maple Grove Cemetery

On the north side of Mason Road, just west of State Route 60 in Vermilion Township, is Maple Grove Cemetery. This large burial ground, which dates to the 1830s, is still in use and actively receives burials.

There are a number of beautifully placed statues throughout the cemetery, though one became quite notorious during the final decades of the twentieth century—the statue of an angel. With its outstretched hands and head inclined to the ground, it stood watch over the burial site of two woman named Lydia and Alice.

According to the legend, this monument was placed to memorialize a mother and daughter. The story claims that the mother had, through some mishap, caused the death of her young child. Overcome with grief, the mother soon followed the girl to the grave.

It wasn't long before area farmers reported strange occurrences in the neighborhood of the cemetery. Livestock began to die off, and children went missing. It was claimed that the statue was coming to life at night

The vandalized angel statue at Maple Grove Cemetery, circa 2001. *Courtesy James A. Willis.*

and roaming the area, causing these disturbances. At this, the hands of the angels and the tips of the wings were removed from the statue to stem its nightly wanderings.

Of course, this legend is completely absurd, as is the backstory. Anyone who takes the time to read the birth and death dates of Alice and Lydia will realize that it would've been impossible for them to have been mother and daughter. The truth is that they were sisters.

Nicholas Fischer came to the United States from Germany in 1854. Six years later, he married Maria Barbara Frolich, and they resided in Vermilion, where he worked as a lumber dealer. No fewer than ten children were born to that union. Among them were the two women who rest beside the angel statue.

Alice Fischer was born in Vermilion on March 16, 1867. She married John J. Humphrey in 1893 and died in Cleveland on January 20, 1921, where she had been living and working as an in-home seamstress. Following her death, a remembrance service was held at her residence, 2003 West 100th Street. She was then interred at Maple Grove Cemetery. She and John had no children.

Lydia Fischer was born in Vermilion on September 10, 1876. She married Conrad H. Nuhn, who was the Erie County treasurer, on January 6, 1903. Lydia died on August 9, 1926, at her home on Elbur Avenue in Lakewood. She was survived by three children: Perry, Alice and Eloise. A fourth child, Betty, died in infancy in 1918.

Shortly after the death of Lydia Nuhn, the statue of the angel was placed at the family burial site in Maple Grove Cemetery. Amos Valentine, an Italian-born sculptor and stone cutter who worked for Lorain Monument

The base that once held the notorious angel statue at Maple Grove Cemetery. *Photo by William G. Krejci.*

Works, carved the brilliant white statue. The names Alice and Lydia were added to the stone base.

As near as can be gleaned, the first damage to the statue occurred on August 13, 1943, when a tornado ripped through Maple Grove Cemetery. Nearly every tree was uprooted, and many of the beautiful memorials were damaged.

During the late 1980s and early 1990s, area high schoolers began to frequently visit the cemetery. During that time, the stories of the bewitched angel statue emerged. Sadly, this resulted in the statue being vandalized. Someone removed the hands and every tip of the feathered wings. The face was painted black, and most of the head was eventually broken off.

The statue has since been removed by Riddle Funeral Home, which maintains the cemetery. It is believed that the damaged remains of the statue are currently being stored in a maintenance building on the grounds of Maple Grove Cemetery. People continue to visit the site and are now vandalizing the pedestal that once held the statue.

THE ABBOTTS' TOMB

Most visitors to the small town of Milan come to view the birthplace of Thomas Edison. Just a few blocks away from the famed inventor's childhood home is Milan Cemetery, where a ghostly couple is said to wander.

The tomb for the Abbott family is built into a hillside at Milan Cemetery. This little mausoleum faces a small pond, making visitation difficult; some say the Abbotts wanted it that way. The front entrance of the tomb is sealed with masonry and block. Still, there is an opening large enough to allow visitors to peer inside. A glimpse through the opening reveals two rusted caskets resting on racks across from each other. Lingering long is not recommended, though, as those who do are reportedly chased off by the ghosts of the Abbott family.

Stories claim that the two caskets in the tomb do not belong to Mr. and Mrs. Abbotts but rather are those of their granddaughters. It's said that Mr. Abbott, in a fit of rage, turned on the little girls and killed them. After he realized his crime, he secretly buried them in a grave on his property. Sometime later, Mr. and Mrs. Abbott passed away and were laid to rest in the tomb. Many years later, the graves of the Abbotts' granddaughters were discovered on the old property. The girls were then moved to the

The Abbotts' Tomb at Milan Cemetery. *Photo by William G. Krejci.*

tomb, and Mr. and Mrs. Abbott were relocated to an adjacent lot. An obelisk marks their burial sites.

And now, the truth.

Benjamin Wright Abbott was born on April 2, 1797, in Rome, New York. At age thirteen, he traveled to Milan with his parents, David and Mary Brown Abbott. His father, commonly known as Squire Abbott, acquired a large farm and built a sizable home on the east side of the Huron River between present-day River Road and Old Mason Road. This house was used as the area's first courthouse and was sometimes referred to as the Old County Seat.

Benjamin Abbott married Lorena Judson, a daughter of Asa and Sarah Minor Judson, on July 11, 1838. They had six children, three of whom died in infancy during an outbreak of epidemic erysipelas in 1843. Sarah Abbott was three at the time of her death. Her twin brothers, Benjamin and Asa, were less than a year old. Since Milan Cemetery was not established until 1851, all three were buried in a small graveyard behind Squire Abbott's home known as the Old County Seat Cemetery.

Benjamin Abbott died on May 6, 1854. It was after his passing that the little family crypt was constructed. It originally faced a small creek (not a pond) and resembled a garden tomb. On March 23, 1865, Benjamin and Lorena's daughter Mary Brown Abbott passed away. She was twenty years old and not married. Three years later, Lorena Abbott died in Wisconsin and was laid to rest in the family tomb, taking her place beside her husband and daughter.

Benjamin and Lorena had two other children, David and Everton. Both men married and had families of their own, but all of their children were born after the passing of Benjamin Abbott, therefore, the story of him killing two granddaughters could not be true. It could be supposed that Benjamin and Lorena's three children who died in 1843 were moved to the tomb in later years, but no evidence exists to support this, either. There are dozens of people still buried at the Old County Seat Cemetery. To move three infants and not the rest of the people, including Benjamin Abbott's parents, doesn't fit the story. Besides, the location of that old burial ground has been forgotten for over a century.

The fact of the matter is that Benjamin and Lorena Abbott, as well as their daughter Mary, are all still interred in the Abbotts' Tomb. The two caskets that sit on the top shelves opposite each other are those of Lorena and Mary, who died in the 1860s. Tucked away on the bottom right-hand side is one more coffin. Benjamin Abbott was originally laid to rest in a wooden coffin. Over the years, time tore that coffin apart, and it has since been encased in brick and mortar.

The floor of the Abbotts' Tomb is littered with plastic flowers and garbage. An old wooden chair sits between the two caskets. It's assumed that Lorena Abbott visited her daughter in the months following her death. This is evidenced by the presence of the chair, as well as the glass window on Mary Brown Abbott's casket. Although it is considered morbid by today's standards, viewing the dead after their departure was not an uncommon practice in the nineteenth century.

The obelisk that stands beside the Abbotts' Tomb doesn't mark the burial place of the Abbott family. It simply gives the names and vital information of those entombed.

Although there were no murdered granddaughters, the tomb of the Abbott family is still believed to be one of the most haunted cemetery sites in Ohio. It certainly is one of the most curious.

CHAPTER VII

CANAL GHOSTS

INTRODUCTION

Prior to the introduction of the railroads, the most effective means for transporting goods over a great distance was by canal. At the peak of their use in the mid-1800s, there were eleven main canals in Ohio that traveled nearly one thousand miles. The first of these great waterways to traverse the state was the Ohio and Erie Canal. Ground was officially broken for this canal on July 4, 1825. Seven years later, the canal was completed. In the end, it traveled just over 308 miles from Cleveland to Portsmouth and contained 143 locks. The northern section began its decline around 1880 with the opening of the Valley Railroad, which ran between Cleveland and Canton. Ohio's canal era officially ended on March 23, 1913, when a great flood decimated the state's canal system.

The first eight stories of this chapter deal with ghostly tales that originated along the Ohio and Erie Canal. These sites are discussed as one would visit them if they were heading south from Cleveland.

WILSON FEED MILL

Located at 7604 Canal Road in Valley View is the Wilson Feed Mill. Erected alongside the Ohio and Erie Canal, this mill is within feet of Lock 37, also called the 14 Mile Lock for the fact that it sits fourteen miles from the northern terminus of the canal. This stately building has borne witness to a colorful history, as well as a legend or two of a haunting.

The Wilson Feed Mill was built in 1855 as a gristmill by brothers Andrew and Robert Alexander and was originally called Alexander's Mill. Their father, James, was an area farmer for whom nearby Alexander Road is named. The wastewater spillage at Lock 37 powered a wooden waterwheel mounted to the side of the mill that turned the large grindstones used for pulverizing grain into flour. The waterwheel was replaced in the late 1800s with a water-powered turbine.

Andrew Alexander continued to operate the mill with his brother until May 1, 1860, when Robert sold his interests. In 1882, Andrew underwent an operation in Cleveland in which one of his eyes had to be removed. Afterward, Andrew's son Clark assisted him with the operation of the mill. Andrew Alexander died in 1895.

In 1900, the old mill was purchased by Thomas and Emma Wilson, who continued to operate the mill and sell grain from an attached store. As demands for flour diminished, the Wilsons focused on selling feed. The mill continued to operate under water power until 1970. Today, it still operates as a feed mill and sells birdseed, pet food and garden supplies.

The majority of the ghost stories about the mill claim that the haunting spirit is that of Andrew Alexander. Many people have reported hearing footsteps in the old place when no one else is about. Some actually claimed to have seen his ghostly form, though none have ever reported seeing a ghost with one eye.

As it turns out, Lock 37 has been the scene of many tragedies.

On the night of Friday, September 30, 1853, a deckhand aboard the canal boat *Gipsey* drowned in the canal. The victim, John Smith, of Cayuga County, New York, was hired at Talmadge the previous evening and was relatively unknown by the crew. As the canal boat approached Lock 37, Smith was sent ahead to make the lock ready for the *Gipsey* to pass through. It's supposed that he slipped and fell into the lock, where he drowned. His remains were taken to Cleveland, where he was buried as an "unknown" in an unmarked grave at Erie Street Cemetery in Section 9, Lot 4, Grave 13.

Just before midnight on Wednesday, September 6, 1876, Captain Charles Stewart of Massillon, owner of the canal boat *Paragon*, accidentally fell overboard at the 14 Mile Lock and drowned. Captain Stewart left behind a wife and several children.

Wilson's Mill, formerly Alexander's Mill, circa 1968. *Library of Congress.*

Two hours after he left the supper table on the evening of August 19, 1911, six-year-old Alfred Jedlicka's body was found wedged in the turbine at Tom Wilson's gristmill. After finishing his dinner, the boy asked his mother if he could go to the old mill, located near their home, and was granted permission. He set off alone but never returned. When Alfred's mother went to search for the boy, she supposed that he might still be at the mill, but Thomas Wilson claimed he had not seen him. This prompted suspicion that the boy had slipped from a bridge spanning the canal and millrace and had fallen in. Wilson drained the millrace, and the boy's lifeless body was recovered.

At around six in the evening on Sunday, June 30, 1912, a family outing turned into a family tragedy. Fred Call of Cleveland was out that day with his brother Phillip and their wives and Fred's son Elmer. Fred had recently repaired his large touring automobile, and this was the family's first outing of the season. As the party approached the Wilson Mill, Fred brought everyone's attention to the peaceful setting of the old mill. He suggested that the women step out and pose for pictures with the mill as a backdrop. After the women exited the vehicle, Fred began to pull the large automobile around but lost control on a treacherous curve; the wheels skidded and sank over the embankment, tossing the car into the canal. Elmer Call was thrown free of the vehicle, but Fred and Phillip were trapped. Phillip managed to keep his head above water until rescuers came to his aid. At first, his brother was thought to have drowned, but after several unsuccessful attempts at resuscitation were made, it was realized that Fred Call broke his neck and was likely killed instantly.

With so many deaths occurring at the site, it's hard to know precisely who would be haunting the old mill and surrounding area.

THE GHOSTS OF THE LONESOME LOCK

Continuing south along the Ohio and Erie Canal, beyond the Village of Boston, we pass through the horseshoe bend at Stumpy Basin and come to a lock in an isolated location. This is Lock 31, most commonly known as the Lonesome Lock, which is regarded by many to be the most haunted lock in Ohio. Tales abound of multiple phantoms at this site, including a headless ghost that's been reported on many occasions. Most claim the haunting can be attributed to the countless number of murders that have occurred there. The place is rich in tales of bandits, thieves, highwaymen and cutthroats. An 1891 newspaper article described the Lonesome Lock thusly:

Near Peninsula is a lock that long since became famous from one end of the canal to the other, and brave indeed is the boatman who even now dares to pass through it after nightfall. For it is a haunted lock. Ghosts and goblins there do congregate. Phantom forms flit about, palpable to the sight, but not to the touch. Fantastic, gruesome tales are told of what the spirits do and have done to those who rashly brave their power.

Old boatmen, wise to the lore that comes with age and experience, shake their heads solemnly when they hear the ghostly tales derided, and to the appreciative listener will tell in hushed and low tones of ghostly presence and power.

Lonesome Lock is alone sufficient to throw something of a romantic glamour about what is mistakenly considered the intensely unromantic canal.

These stories are reinforced by a canal boat captain from the nineteenth century named Lorenzo "Doc" Seeley. In regard to Lock 31, he recalled that a man was said to have had his head chopped off there. The headless body of the man was believed to roam about the lock each night looking for its missing crown. Superstitious boatmen refused to pass through the lock at night and would tie up in either Boston or Peninsula and take the delay rather than face the headless ghost.

Regarding murders having taken place at Lonesome Lock, it's claimed that more than a dozen people have met their end there, but very little evidence exists to support this. No newspaper article could be located regarding murders at Lock 31. The only story about this comes from an old canal boat captain named Pearl Nye.

Captain Nye recalled that a man from Akron named Loren Perry was taking the canal boat *Narragansett* through Lonesome Lock. As he approached, he heard some men talking about throwing someone into the lock. After being startled by Perry, the men scattered. There, on the ground, was the body of a man who'd been brutally murdered. Perry and his crew decided to leave the body where they found it and reported the murder once they reached Boston.

The only other fantastic story that Captain Nye related regarding the Lonesome Lock is about a haunted house that once stood near the site. People claimed to see the apparition of a mysterious jack-o'-lantern at the old place.

Curiously, the tale of a headless spirit has been altered in recent years, changing the ghost from a man to a woman. In the new telling, a woman was decapitated at the site around 1850, and her body was cast into the canal. Just as with her male predecessor, her headless ghost is said to wander the lock at night.

In truth, an incident happened very close to the Lonesome Lock that involved a man being nearly beheaded. On the evening of August 18, 1886, Thomas H. Reed, a former Cleveland councilman, was returning from the Republican Congressional Convention in Akron on the Valley Railroad. While on the platform passing between two cars, Reed leaned out for but a moment—that was all it took. The train was approaching the bridge over the Cuyahoga River just to the north of Peninsula, beyond a cut through the hillside called Devil's Pass. Reed's head struck the bridge's trestle, and his body was thrown from the train. He was killed almost instantly. The train was moving at a fast rate and took nearly a quarter mile to stop before it backed up to recover the body. All of this occurred within sight of the Lonesome Lock.

A view of Lock 31, famously known as Lonesome Lock, circa 1892. *Courtesy Cuyahoga Valley National Park.*

A present-day view of Lonesome Lock from the same location. *Photo by William G. Krejci.*

There may be yet another reason for the haunting of Lonesome Lock. It's said that for every mile of canal, there sits a canal-digger's grave. Lonesome Lock is no exception. In another article from 1891, clues are given as to the location of the site of a number of forgotten and unmarked burials. The article, which describes the canal between Boston and Peninsula, states that this site is near the horseshoe bend, on the bank amid the woods, at a lonely spot. These graves appear in the form of a number of low hillocks that are easily overlooked.

The horseshoe bend at Stumpy Basin is a wetland that's a perfect breeding ground for disease-carrying mosquitoes but not an ideal location to bury those who died of the swamp fever they carried. Lock 31 sits just beyond on higher ground. The answer to the question of why these men were buried under mounds and not in traditional pits is an easy one. The site was among the trees, where roots would hinder digging efforts. The canal ditch was being constructed nearby. It would've proved much easier to simply cover these men with earth excavated from the canal.

A recent trip to Lonesome Lock revealed these mounds as still in existence, within sight of the canal, and—just as the writer of the 1891 article described them—at a lonely spot.

These recently rediscovered mounds, located just southwest of Lonesome Lock, contain the remains of canal diggers who died of swamp fever in 1826. *Photo by William G. Krejci.*

DEEP LOCK AND QUARRY

Just south of State Route 303 on Riverview Road in Peninsula sits Deep Lock Quarry Metro Park. This park was established in 1934, shortly after the quarry closed. The quarry itself was established a little over one hundred years earlier, when sandstone was pulled from the site for use in the construction of canal locks. Located within the park is Lock 28, also known as Deep Lock, which had the greatest elevation change on the Ohio and Erie Canal. Most locks raised or lowered a canal boat nine feet. The appropriately named Deep Lock had an elevation change of seventeen feet.

Visitors claim to hear the anguished voices of men killed in the many quarrying accidents believed to have occurred at the site. The lock itself is said to be haunted by canal-diggers who died during the lock's construction. The facts tell a different story.

On the morning of Sunday, November 8, 1863, the canal boat *Massillon Mills* was southbound from Cleveland. As it approached Lock 28, a twenty-seven-year-old crewman named Leonard Friend, of Tuscarawas Township, Stark County, was sent ahead to prepare the lock. While getting the lock

Deep Lock Quarry, 1890s. *Courtesy Peninsula Library & Historical Society.*

Deep Lock in Peninsula, 1890s. *Courtesy Peninsula Library & Historical Society.*

A present-day view of Deep Lock from the same location. *Photo by William G. Krejci.*

ready for the boat to enter, he slipped and fell into the canal. Friend called out for help, but before the crew could reach him, he'd gone under, and he never resurfaced.

On the afternoon of November 7, 1887, a five-year-old daughter of the Bell family, who lived near Deep Lock, had taken a piece of bread and went outside to play along the towpath. At around 3:00 p.m., her mother went out to look for her. She found the piece of bread, but the child was nowhere to be seen. A search was organized with neighbors, and the child's body was discovered in the canal.

In terms of fatal accidents that have occurred in the quarry, only one could be verified. That accident occurred on the afternoon of October 8, 1890. While removing a large stone from the excavation point, a large derrick that was being used to hoist the block failed and sent the entire works crashing down. Two men were killed by the falling wreckage. John Wagner was just forty years old and had come to work at the quarry only two weeks earlier. He left behind a wife and four children. Very little is known about John Mullins, the other man who was killed. Wagner was buried at Cedar Grove Cemetery in Peninsula. No burial information can be found for Mullins. It may be that there was nothing left to bury.

JOHNNYCAKE LOCK

The next lock to the south of Deep Lock is Lock 27, also known as Johnnycake Lock. It received its curious name as a result of an incident that happened in 1828. That spring, there was a severe flood. Silt and debris were washed down Furnace Run, which fed the newly completed canal at that point, creating an obstruction. A number of canal boats were stranded at the site for many days, and their passengers and crews survived on cornmeal pancakes known as johnnycakes. Shortly thereafter, the small village was called Johnny Cake Lock. The name was eventually changed to Unionville and was changed again, around 1880, to Everett.

The most popular ghost story about Johnnycake Lock concerns the spirit of a young boy. Legends claim that a child named Henry accidentally drowned while swimming in the canal, though no evidence of Henry exists. The only known death to have occurred at Johnnycake Lock happened on July 24, 1874. An article from the *Akron Daily Argus* reported:

The ruins of Johnnycake Lock, February 1962. *Courtesy Peninsula Library & Historical Society.*

On Friday afternoon, just as the canal boat Twilight *went into Johnny Cake Lock, about 12 miles north of the city, a little child of the cook on the boat, about two years and a half old, in some manner fell into the water and was drowned. Mr. Merchant, the father of the child, also employed on the boat, jumped in after it, and, in his efforts to save the life of the child, nearly lost his own. The body was soon afterward recovered, and arrived on the boat on Saturday afternoon, when a coffin was procured, and at 5 o'clock, the funeral of the child took place from Lock 1.*

Though no first names are given, evidence points to this being a daughter of George and Julia Merchant of Cincinnati.

Akron Civic Theatre

Located along the Ohio and Erie Canal in Akron is one of the grandest theater houses in Ohio. The elegance of its decor is rivaled by no other in the Buckeye State. Here, too, stories of ghostly encounters abound. No one said that a canal ghost had to resign itself to the canal alone. Why would it when a building of this magnitude crosses over the ditch itself?

Initial construction began on the Akron Civic Theatre in April 1918. This was to be a massive complex called the Hippodrome, but after completion of the lobby, the project was abandoned. In 1922, a rejuvenation began with the announcement that Cleveland interests were going to finish the project by constructing a 3,200-seat theater. This was to be leased to Loew's Ohio Theaters, Inc. Famed architect John Eberson was contracted for the job, and the work was completed just in time for the start of the 1929 season.

The atmospheric auditorium was designed to emulate the courtyard and gardens of a Moorish castle. Surrounding the perimeter of the hall are many architectural details that resemble roof lines. As the house lights come down, the ceiling comes to life as a soft sunset. Moviegoers who glance away from the on-screen feature may have been dazzled to see stars upon the ceiling as well as the occasional passing cloud (created by a cloud projector).

One of the crowning jewels was the 1929 three-manual, nineteen-rank Wurlitzer theater organ. This was primarily used to accompany silent movies, but with the advent of "talkies," use of this instrument shifted to concerts.

Interestingly, the Ohio and Erie Canal runs under a section of the building that connects the original Hippodrome lobby with the auditorium.

The haunting of the Akron Civic Theatre is primarily attributed to three restless spirits. The first is simply known as Fred. It's believed that Fred was a janitor during the days of the Loew's occupancy. The story is that Fred passed away during his shift and now returns to watch over the place. Some claim that he gets particularly upset with anyone who messes up the restrooms. This may simply be a cautionary tale relayed in an attempt to keep the facilities clean.

The second reported specter is that of a well-dressed man who occupies the balcony. His identity can scarcely be known, but he's believed to be either a former patron or a vaudeville actor who used to perform at the theater.

The last ghost is supposedly a woman who committed suicide by jumping into the canal. Her spirit is said to roam the canal below the theater. Most reports place her death as occurring at Lock 3, though it's actually Lock 4 that adjoins the theater site.

The Akron Civic Theatre, circa 1934. *Reprinted with permission of the* Akron Beacon Journal *and Ohio.com.*

In the course of my research on the Akron Civic Theatre, I couldn't locate files or records concerning the death of a janitor named Fred or any connection to the death of a well-dressed man. These are likely urban legends. However, there were a number of deaths and suicides at Lock 4. The earliest of these occurred at 3:30 in the afternoon on September 21,

1882. Mike Moore, a man of about fifty-five, had fallen from the canal boat *Ocean* into the canal at Lock 4 and drowned. It was noted that Moore was intoxicated at the time but was also subject to seizures, one of which he reportedly suffered at the time of his death.

November 22, 1883, was the date of the accidental drowning of twelve-year-old Jacob Waickmann, who was carrying milk from Christy's Tannery to his home at 121 Bowery Street. While crossing the canal at Lock 4, he noticed an approaching canal boat. He set down the pail of milk and assisted in opening the lock. It was determined that he must have slipped into the canal while handling the large paddles that opened the gates, but nobody noticed him going into the water. A boat passing through the lock some time later brought his hat to the surface. An alarm went out, and a crowd assembled. The body was recovered by William Viers, an employee at a nearby mill.

Also of note is the suicide of twenty-four-year-old Edward F. Moore of Minerva, Ohio (no relation to the previously mentioned Mike Moore). Edward Moore had inherited $426 from his father's estate and made his way to Akron, where he became a habitual drunkard. After only sixty days in Akron, Edward Moore was penniless and told acquaintances that they should soon find his body in that town. The women with whom he kept company last saw him on the night of St. Patrick's Day, 1885, near Lock 4. Afterward, they made inquiries concerning his whereabouts but to no avail. His body was recovered from the canal that April.

December 21, 1890, was the date of the recovery of the body of John Moon, an unwed street paver originally from Ireland. It was believed that he was drunk when he went into the canal. Some suspected that he'd committed suicide, but the coroner listed his cause of death as drowning.

Henry Huber, a fifty-three-year-old grocer from Akron, drowned at Lock 4 on July 13, 1896. The incident was witnessed by two people, a young boy named Armstead Dickson and Mrs. Chaffee. Both were of the opinion that he'd committed suicide by jumping into the canal from the middle of the gates. Members of his family, however, suggested that he'd suffered from fits of dizziness and was probably seized by one while walking across the lock. He left behind a wife and nine children. The coroner ruled it an accidental drowning.

Please take note that none of these drownings in the canal at the site of the Akron Civic Theatre involve a woman, as the ghost stories claim.

Tragedies that occurred on the site extend well beyond these sad drownings. The most prominent occurred on the evening of August 22,

1900, at the City Building and Columbia Hall, which stood on the site prior to the construction of the Akron Civic Theatre.

The story begins with the arrest of Louis H. Peck, a black man, on the charge of assaulting a six-year-old white girl named Tina Maas. Peck claimed that he was in Youngstown at the time of the supposed assault but was coerced into confessing. Once he was charged, word circulated throughout Akron that a lynch mob was forming. That afternoon, Akron police had Peck, as well as another black man named William Howard, moved to Cleveland for safety. Howard had been arrested earlier on a different charge, but the police thought it best not to keep him at the jail in case he was mistaken for Peck.

At 7:30 that evening, a mob consisting of hundreds of men converged on the city prison, located in the City Building, with the intent of lynching Peck. They rushed the entrance and were met with little resistance. After it was determined that Peck was not at the city prison, the mob descended upon the city jail two blocks away. Not finding him there, either, the mob made its way to the courthouse next door, where a search was made, but again, Peck could not be located. The angry mob returned to the city prison and forced another entry by using a battering ram. By 10:00 p.m., the mob had swelled to more than a thousand people.

In an attempt to disperse the mob, police officers fired shots over their heads. At this, the mob picked up bricks, rocks and guns of their own and opened fire upon the officers. Caught in the crossfire was Glen Wade, the eleven-year-old son of Lillian Wade, an employee of the nearby Empire Hotel. He was shot through the heart and died instantly.

Shortly afterward, John M. Davidson, a merchant and coal dealer, was hurrying past the scene in an open carriage with his family. His wife, Minnie, was riding on the seat beside him. In her arms was their sleeping seven-year-old daughter Rhoda Ella Davidson. The crowd had retreated across the street but was continuing their assault upon the City Building. A police officer discharged his revolver in the direction of the mob, but his bullet struck Rhoda Davidson through the temple. She died of her injury two days later.

The riot raged on through the night, with the mob setting off multiple sticks of dynamite in front of the City Building and Columbia Hall. By dawn, the crowd had dispersed. In the end, two children lay dead and eighteen people were severely injured. City Hall, City Jail, the City Building and the prison were all in ruins. Columbia Hall, two saloons and several business blocks had burned to the ground.

Columbia Hall and City Building after the Akron Riot of 1900. *Reprinted with permission of the* Akron Beacon Journal *and Ohio.com.*

Three days after the riot, Peck was returned to Akron in secret, and a rushed trial was held. He was found guilty of assaulting Tina Maas and was sentenced to life in prison. On October 5, 1900, forty-five men were indicted for their part in the August riot. The charges included burglary, larceny, rioting, arson, shooting with intent to kill and wound and unlawful possession and use of dynamite.

Incidentally, it was later determined that the assault upon Tina Maas was fabricated and Peck was innocent. He was pardoned and released from prison in May 1913.

No one can say for certain who or what haunts the Akron Civic Theatre, but with so much tragedy concentrated upon that site, it would be a surprise if it wasn't haunted.

CLINTON GUARD LOCK MILL

On the south side of Akron, near Portage Lakes, the Ohio and Erie Canal joins with the Tuscarawas River and departs the Great Lakes watershed. A few miles southwest of Akron, the canal approaches the sleepy village of Clinton, where a ghost story has been forgotten for nearly 140 years.

This tale centers around a man named Gorham Chapin, who was born on March 16, 1795, in Bernardston, Massachusetts, to Dr. Caleb and Mary Wright Chapin. Gorham served as a private in Longley's Regiment of the Massachusetts Militia during the War of 1812 and was stationed at Boston. During the 1820s, he resided in Buffalo with his uncle, Dr. Cyrenius Chapin, who was a hero of note during that same war.

In the early 1830s, Gorham Chapin traveled to Ohio and settled in Clinton, which was then located on the west bank of the Tuscarawas River. It was at Clinton that the Ohio and Erie Canal crossed the Tuscarawas on a pond of still water created by a dam in the river. Just south of the crossing, the canal passed through a unique type of lock called a guard lock. This served to control the amount of water entering the canal and also protected the canal and the village of Clinton from flooding.

In 1835, Gorham Chapin crossed the river, and laid out a new village near the guard lock that he named Orradeen. Two years later, another village was established on the lots to the south and called Pumroy. Eventually, the names Orradeen and Pumroy were abandoned, and the area was named Clinton.

The Guard Lock at Clinton. Gorham Chapin's sawmill once sat in the woods to the right. *Photo by William G. Krejci.*

When he laid out his village, Gorham Chapin also established a sawmill along the wastewater that spilled around the guard lock. By accounts, it was considered a rather good mill with reaction wheels but spent much time sitting idle due to a lack of water caused by frequent breaks in the dam.

Gorham Chapin died at Clinton on October 15, 1841. By 1854, ghost stories about the old sawmill were circulating, with claims that Chapin's ghost could be heard filing the saw blades "amid the fitful gusts of midnight, when ghosts most love to walk abroad." An 1881 retelling of this states:

> *After Mr. Chapin died in 1841, his old mill is said to have been haunted. Strange sounds are said to have been heard there by those who had occasion to pass the old mill during the solemn hours of the night. It was said by the credulous that Mr. Chapin's ghost would wander into the mill, and a strange noise like the filing of a saw thrilled the hearts of listeners.*

The site of the Clinton Guard Lock Mill is in the swampy woods to the east of the old Guard Lock ruins. No trace of the mill exists today. Interestingly, this site is within view of the storied crybaby bridge at Clinton.

WAREHOUSE ON THE CANAL

Ghost stories are nothing new at Canal Fulton. In 1881 and 1882, the *Cleveland Plain Dealer* reported on at least two hauntings in that town. One of these was at a church where the ghost was said to play the organ. Those stories may have been forgotten, but one haunting has gained popularity. Located at 239 North Canal Street is the Warehouse on the Canal. In a stark contrast to the haunting of the Clinton Guard Lock Mill, just three and a half miles to the north, reports of paranormal activity at the old warehouse are fairly recent and don't appear to predate the early 2000s, when the building was renovated.

The story of the haunted warehouse begins in early 1902, when brothers James and Charles Finefrock purchased the Daily Furniture Company in Canal Fulton. Both men had previously worked as schoolteachers but were looking to enter private industry. Charles R. Daily started his furniture company in 1894 and also operated a mortuary. The furniture company and mortuary were reorganized and by July 1902 were operating under

Built as the Finefrock Building in 1906, the Warehouse on the Canal housed a furniture store and mortuary. *Photo by William G. Krejci.*

the name Finefrock Brothers, with James running the store and Charles working as the salesman.

In early 1906, construction commenced on a new office, store, warehouse and mortuary parlor for the Finefrocks. The company moved into the new building in early December of that year. In 1924, James Finefrock's son-in-law Paul R. Swigart took over the firm's funerary operations. Two years later, James and Charles Finefrock dissolved their partnership. Charles relocated to Massillon and opened his own furniture company. He went on to become one of that city's most revered civic leaders.

James Finefrock died on April 1, 1936. The following year, the Swigarts moved the funeral operations to their residence at 624 East Cherry Street in Canal Fulton, where it continues operating to this day as the Swigart-Easterling Funeral Home.

Aside from cold spots, doors opening and closing and mysterious lights, visitors have reported seeing ghostly people dressed in period attire consistent with the early twentieth century.

LOCK 4 PARK

One mile south of Canal Fulton sits Lock 4 Park. The most popular legend states that while the lock was being built, a foreman was told that the operation was to be shut down and that his position was terminated. In a fit of rage, he grabbed a large container of acid and cast it upon his coworkers, killing some and horrifically disfiguring others. He then dumped the acid upon himself, ending his own life. His wicked ghost is said to roam about the lock at night.

Another story states that he wasn't a foreman but a lock tender who rented that section of the canal from the government. Similarly, it's stated that he was to be terminated, and the incident with the acid occurred, but now he also haunts the old lock tender's house at Lock 4 Park.

Both of these stories are highly suspect. To begin with, large amounts of acid weren't readily available during the canal era, nor were they usually kept where they could be easily obtained and thrown "in a fit of rage." Furthermore, there was never a time during the construction of the Ohio and Erie Canal during which operations were to be shut down. As far as the second story is concerned, most locks on the Ohio and Erie Canal were tended by the crew of the canal boats and not lock tenders. To further discredit this second version, the lock tender's house at Lock 4 Park was built as a Works Progress Administration project in the 1930s and didn't exist when the canal was in operation.

So, what's the true story?

Lock 4 Park was once the site of a small village called Fenelon. In 1832, a man named James Duncan built a four-story wooden gristmill upon the site and attempted to develop a new city there. His plans fell short of his expectations. Six years earlier, Duncan had successfully founded the city of Massillon, which he'd named for a French bishop who lived during the reign of King Louis XIV. The new settlement of Fenelon was named for another French bishop who served during that same era. Development never took off, as most people preferred nearby Massillon or Canal Fulton. Aside from the gristmill, a tavern house was also located at Fenelon along the canal at Lock 4. This was owned by Samuel Zimmerman of Wayne County.

Duncan only operated the gristmill at Fenelon for a few years before selling it off. It changed hands many times before it ceased operations in 1888. It was ultimately torn down in early 1908. The last family to operate the gristmill was the Harmons. Their descendants signed over the former mill lot in 1938 to the State Division of Conservation to create Lock 4 Park.

Lock 4 in Canal Fulton is said to be haunted by a foreman or lock tender who burned himself and others with acid. Photo circa 1948. *Courtesy Cleveland Public Library Photograph Collection.*

As far as murders are concerned, only one from that area is recorded.

On the afternoon of Saturday, August 15, 1874, a thirty-five-year-old man from Massillon named Peter Paier traveled to Canal Fulton to withdraw money from the bank. He was accompanied by three men: Augustus Cribblez, Edward Miller and Louis Prater. After withdrawing the money, which exceeded $1,000, the group visited several saloons. During the evening, one of the men drugged Paier by slipping laudanum into his drink. After the authorities were informed of the incident, a search was made, and the men were discovered on the outskirts of Canal Fulton, where they were taken into custody. A physician was sent for, but Paier was beyond saving. He died at 4:00 a.m. Peter Paier was to be married that Monday morning. Instead, he was buried.

The men claimed that they'd been trying to keep Paier from spending his money at the saloons and were attempting to get him back to Massillon. To accomplish this, they visited a druggist and acquired the bottle of laudanum, hoping to knock Paier out and get him on the train. None of them were aware that it could kill him. As it wasn't their intention to kill Paier, only incapacitate him, both Miller and Cribblez were convicted of manslaughter the following year and served time for their offense. Louis Prater, who neither purchased the laudanum nor put it into Paier's drink, was not charged.

BUCKLIN'S LOCK

While the Ohio and Erie Canal crossed the state to the east, the Miami and Erie Canal did so to the west. Ground was broken on that canal only a couple of weeks after the start of the Ohio and Erie, but it would be twenty years before it saw its completion, traveling 250 miles from Toledo to Cincinnati. The northern section between Toledo and the small town of Junction also carried the easternmost section of the Wabash and Erie Canal, which ran to Evansville, Indiana, covering a distance of more than 460 miles, making it the longest canal in North America. Like its counterpart in the east, the Miami and Erie Canal met its demise during the great flood of 1913.

Just across the Maumee River from Grand Rapids, Ohio, sits Providence Metropark. Within its boundaries are the Isaac Ludwig Mill and Lock 44, which is one of the last working locks in the state. Guests can enjoy a one-hour excursion through the lock and a restored section of the canal aboard the *Volunteer*, a reproduction mule-drawn canal boat.

About two miles to the west along Old U.S. Route 24 is a pull-off beside the ruins of an old lock. Lock 43 on the Miami and Erie Canal was more famously known as Bucklin's Lock. It received this name from Charles Bucklin, who settled the area in the early 1800s. At first glance, it appears to be just another lock with nothing spectacular about it. In truth, it's the scene of a mysterious haunting that has been forgotten for over one hundred years.

A 1902 newspaper article reported on the ghostly guardian of the lock, stating that canal boat crews approaching Bucklin's Lock would see a man with a long white beard standing at the lock ahead of them. After pausing for a moment, he would open the gate to let the boat enter. The crew would hail him, but he never answered; he'd simply turn away and walk off into the misty gloom. As the boat reached the lock, the crew found it to be closed again.

Others witnessed a man pacing along the bank of the canal after nightfall or heard his wailing cries in the darkness. When the sounds were investigated, no source was discovered. What could be the cause of this otherworldly visitation? The author of the article ascribes the restless spirit as being the ghost of a man who died at the site many years earlier.

William Bellinger was born in Maumee in 1825. In December 1854, he married Polly Ann Welcott, but the marriage was a short one, as she died soon after. He married again in January 1857 to Jerusha Jane Cozins, with whom he had nine children. William Bellinger enlisted in Cleveland as a private with the Union army in March 1864 and was assigned to the 10th Ohio Independent Company Sharpshooters. Several months later, he was wounded in battle and sent to White Hall Hospital in Pennsylvania, where he was discharged on May 19, 1865.

According to family history, William and Jerusha Bellinger moved to the small village of Texas, Ohio, on the Maumee River in 1866, where William worked as a ferryman. It's said that he was a heavy drinker and that his wife, after assembling a group of women from the local Methodist church, smashed up the local saloon in an attempt to keep him sober.

William Bellinger worked as the ferryman at Texas as late as 1886 but soon after was living at nearby Bucklin's Lock, where he worked as a lock tender. His family remained in Texas, while he stayed by himself at the lock in an old converted icehouse in the woods.

On October 18, 1887, canal superintendent Meecham passed through the area, paying off the employees of the canal. He paid William Bellinger three months' wages in silver. Bellinger was seen tending to his duties at Bucklin's Lock that afternoon and evening but came up missing the following morning. A search was made, and it was discovered that the old icehouse had been burned to the ground. The charred remains of William Bellinger were located after the search party pried up some debris in the wreckage.

An investigation into the death of William Bellinger was conducted, but the results were inconclusive. A number of suspicious men were seen in the area the day before his death, and it was supposed that he might have met his end through foul play. His three months' wages in silver were never located in the debris.

Several months after his death, reports started to come in regarding a ghostly lock tender at Bucklin's Lock. Many supposed it to be William Bellinger returning to tend to his former duties. The haunting of Bucklin's Lock was said to have continued for many years.

GRETCHEN'S LOCK

As stated in the chapter regarding the Bowman Cemetery witch, ground was broken for the Sandy and Beaver Canal in 1834. It was completed in 1848 and traveled from Bolivar, Ohio, to Glasgow, Pennsylvania. Along the way, it passed through two tunnels. The longest of these extended 1,600 yards, making it the longest canal tunnel in North America. The canal's existence was short-lived. It closed in 1852 following the failure of a reservoir dam.

Nestled among the high sandstone cliffs near Sprucevale are the remains of Lock 41 on the Sandy and Beaver Canal. This lock bears the name Gretchen's Lock. Stories claim that Gretchen was a young daughter of the canal's chief engineer, Edward Gill.

When the Gill family was coming to the United States from Holland in 1834, Gill's wife passed away on the voyage and was buried at sea. Young Gretchen followed her mother to the grave on August 12, 1838, when she died from malaria. Edward Gill had his daughter's remains interred in a small tomb that he'd built into Lock 41. Later that year, Gill returned to Europe, bringing Gretchen's coffin with him. On the voyage across the Atlantic, the ship sank, reuniting the family that had been separated four years earlier. Many people claim to see Gretchen's ghost wandering about the site of the lock that bears her name. The story is so famous that it's the subject of a song by Westside Steve Simmons called "The Ballad of Gretchen's Lock."

It's a fantastic story, although not a single a word is true.

The ruins of Gretchen's Lock at Beaver Creek State Park. *Photo by William G. Krejci.*

Edward Hall Gill was born in Enniscorthy, County Wexford, Ireland, on January 20, 1806. In 1814, the family relocated to Halifax, Nova Scotia. Three years later, the Gills moved to Herkimer, New York, where Edward's father, Valentine, was employed as an engineer on the Erie Canal. Edward joined his father in that venture and soon began working as an assistant engineer. Upon completion of the Erie Canal, Edward Gill worked as an engineer on other canal projects in Delaware, Georgia and Pennsylvania.

In 1834, Edward Gill came to Ohio and was employed as chief engineer on the Sandy and Beaver Canal project, though he did not spend much time in Ohio. In 1838, he moved to Richmond, Virginia, and was employed as an engineer on many canal projects and as superintendent of numerous railroads. In early 1868, he suffered a stroke that left him paralyzed. Edward Hall Gill died on December 20, 1868, and was laid to rest two days later at Hollywood Cemetery in Richmond.

According to the facts, Edward Gill was eleven years old when he arrived in the United States. This contradicts the story of him coming over from Holland in 1834 with a daughter. Obviously, he would have been too young to have had a daughter, let alone a wife that died on the voyage. Gill was married by 1850 to a woman named Mary, though no evidence exists to support the idea that they had a daughter named Gretchen.

Mary Gill died in 1870 and was buried beside her husband. Close investigation of their burial site at Hollywood Cemetery revealed a third grave, located beside Edward and Mary Gill, that contains the remains of a little girl who was buried on March 4, 1856. Findagrave.com lists the child as being Mary Gill, but further investigation showed this to be Alice Ruffen Gill, a three-year-old daughter of Edward's younger brother, Washington.

As far as Gretchen's Lock is concerned, there is a small nook in the stonework. Is it a tomb? Not likely.

The first mention of this in print appeared in the book *Ohio and Pennsylvania Reminiscences* by Ira Mansfield, which was released in 1916. In the book, Mansfield refers to it as "Little Gretchen's Cache." In fact, it is not referred to as being a tomb until 1952, when Max Gard and William Vodrey released their book *The Sandy and Beaver Canal*. Here, they called it an open crypt that once held Gretchen's coffin. A 1973 newspaper article places Gretchen's death in the early fall of 1836. It also says that the family was from Switzerland. Gretchen's death date of August 12, 1838, first appears in the 1991 book *Haunted Ohio* by Chris Woodyard. That book also named Gretchen's father as being Gill Hans.

Some experts on the history of the Sandy and Beaver Canal suspect that Gretchen may not have been a little girl at all but was instead a mule that worked the area of Lock 41. So, if young Gretchen never existed, who is the little girl that haunts the lock?

THE TRAGEDY OF JAKE'S LOCK

Not far from Gretchen's Lock sits another famed ghostly lock. Jake's Lock is rumored to be haunted by the spirit of a former lock tender named Jake. The story says that Jake was working the lock late one night in the middle of a terrible thunderstorm. Poor Jake was struck by lightning and thrown into the canal. Some stories claim that he was electrocuted, while others say he drowned. Much like the specter at Bucklin's Lock, Jake continues to roam the site, but his presence is quite a grisly one—he appears as a charred man holding a lantern.

Something of a controversy at the center of this story is the actual location of Jake's Lock. Some claim that Jake's Lock is the crumbling lock

Lock 42 at the ghost town of Sprucevale was the setting for the Tragedy of Jake's Lock. *Photo by William G. Krejci.*

that sits in Sprucevale within sight of Hambleton's Mill. A 1994 book by Linn Loomis claims that Lock 39, located deep in the woods beyond Gretchen's Lock, is actually Jake's Lock, while the one at Sprucevale, Lock 42, is Hambleton's Lock.

The truth of the matter is that historically speaking, Jake's Lock doesn't exist. According to Ray Hall of the Sandy and Beaver Canal Association, longtime canal association secretary Ellen Herman actually wrote the story of Jake's Lock in 1979 as a short play that the association put on to raise money for the refurbishment of Lock 36 in Pioneer Village. The play about Jake was performed at Lock 42 in Sprucevale, with Tom Miller playing the role of Jake. According to Herman's story, that's where her fictional Jake was killed.

Herman says that the story she wrote about Jake does have some basis in historical fact, but the original events occurred on the Ohio and Erie Canal, not on the Sandy and Beaver.

So, concerning the location controversy, is "Jake's Lock" Lock 39 or Lock 42? It doesn't matter. Jake never existed.

CHAPTER VIII

GORE ORPHANAGE

THE LEGEND OF GORE ORPHANAGE

The final section of this book reveals the true and complete story of one of Northern Ohio's most famous ghostly legends, that of Gore Orphanage. The tale has evolved over the years, with many aspects being altered. In every version, the orphanage is portrayed as something out of a Charles Dickens novel. Recently, it's been used as the backdrop of a few independent films and was even the setting of an episode of the television series *Supernatural.* Anyone who's familiar with Gore Orphanage is sure to have heard at least one version of this tale.

The original legend claims that in the early 1800s, there was an old man named Gore who built an orphanage on the western edge of Lorain County. He was an abusive man who strictly adhered to the rule "spare the rod, spoil the child." In later years, the orphanage was losing money. Facing destitution, Gore developed a sinister plan. One night, he locked the doors with the orphans inside and splashed the base of the building with lantern oil. He set it ablaze and watched as the trapped orphans burned to death. Afterward, he collected the insurance money and left town. It's said that visitors to the site often hear the ghostly children crying in the night.

Modern versions of this tale are somewhat different. Thanks to advances in research technology, a slightly more honest tale has emerged. This updated version tells that the place was actually called the Light of Hope Orphanage.

It opened around the turn of the century and only operated for a few years. The administrator was Reverend Sprunger, who was almost as abusive as the legendary Gore. Some say that a few children met their end at his hand and that gravestones exist beside the river. In this later adaptation, the orphanage burned down on accident. In both versions, visitors to the site can hear the late-night cries of burning orphans.

The most recent telling states that there was no devastating fire that claimed the lives of children. A print shop on the grounds burned, but there were no injuries. One supposed expert on the story claimed that the tale was based on the tragic Collinwood school fire in Cleveland. This expert also said that nothing bad ever happened at the site of the orphanage. Historic facts say otherwise.

The true story may simply be a case of the best laid plans of mice and men going astray. You be the judge.

THE SPRUNGERS

So, who was this villainous Reverend Sprunger who operated the ill-fated orphanage? The true story may surprise you.

Johann Abraham (John) Sprunger was born in Berne, Switzerland, on August 12, 1852. Two years later, he immigrated with his family to the United States and settled in Berne, Indiana, where as he joined the Mennonite church. Early in life, he was involved in various businesses, including a hardware store, lumber company, hotel and drugstore. On February 15, 1880, he married his first cousin Katharina Sprunger. Later that year, their first child, a daughter named Hillegonda, was born. In 1884, Katharina gave birth to a stillborn child named Edmund, whom they buried at the First Mennonite Church Cemetery. Three years later, Hillegonda died unexpectedly and was laid to rest beside her brother.

Katharina and John Sprunger. *Courtesy Vermilion History Museum.*

In 1889, the Sprungers returned to Switzerland, where they learned about the Deaconess movement of fostering children. It was at that time that John was ordained as a Mennonite minister. While there, Katharina had another child who was stillborn. The Sprungers returned to Indiana in 1890, and the following year, their son Salem was born. Sadly, his life was short. He died a year later and was interred beside his brother and sister.

THE FIRST ORPHANAGE

Shortly after returning to Indiana, the Sprungers ordained a number of women as deaconesses and established the Light of Hope Society. These women traveled to Chicago and worked as missionaries. On April 1, 1893, the Light of Hope Orphanage opened in Berne, Indiana, with the admission of two children from Chicago named Leo and Josephine. Over the next few years, additions were constructed on the facility to accommodate the growing number of children.

In the early morning hours of April 19, 1899, a fire broke out on the third floor of the girls' dormitory, which was called Jerusalem. Most of the children were able to escape through a window to the roof of a second-floor portico, but three of them weren't as lucky. According to the newspapers, the girls who were killed were fourteen-year-old Katie Dibble Baker of Cleveland, fifteen-year-old Mamie Braddick of Chicago, and a seven-year-old girl named Delia Taylor from Linn Grove, Illinois. All three girls were found near each other. A fourth victim named Katie Goble was reported to have died a few days later from injuries sustained after jumping from a window. Different variations of these names appeared in many newspaper accounts, so the names may not be entirely accurate. No burial information exists for these children, which makes identifying their families even more difficult. They were likely laid to rest at the First Mennonite Church Cemetery in Berne.

The cause of the fire was traced to a stove on the third floor. After the fire, the dormitory was rebuilt, but the orphanage closed and relocated a few years later due to the fact that it had outgrown the facility. Later statements claimed that the move was a result of friction between Reverend Sprunger and the citizens of Berne over his poor management of the institution.

LORAIN COUNTY

In 1903, John Sprunger, through the title of the Children's Rescue Society, purchased approximately five hundred acres of farmland in Brownhelm and Henrietta Townships in western Lorain County. Some have claimed that the road bisecting this property was called Gore Road. That name wasn't applied until many years later.

The institution was composed of many different farms. The caretaker's house was built years earlier by William Denman. Nearby was a three-story building that was used as a print shop for the publishing of the organization's newsletter, the *Light of Hope Monthly*. At the top of the hill to the south and east was the boys' home in the original Hughes house. The girls' school was located farther east in the former Joseph Howard home.

After the Sprunger family moved to Vermilion, Hillegonda Sprunger's remains were exhumed from the First Mennonite Church Cemetery and reinterred on the grounds of the new orphanage.

The facility, which housed around 120, was primarily an agricultural school that taught farming. Other trades and lessons were also taught, as

The boys' home at the Light of Hope Orphanage. *From* Lorain County, Ohio: Picturesque and Industrial Features.

The girls' school at the Light of Hope Orphanage. *From* Lorain County, Ohio: Picturesque and Industrial Features.

the orphanage had two elementary school teachers and a music teacher. Children, whether they were orphaned or not, were welcomed at the home. Their ages ranged between two and seventeen, and all ethnicities were welcomed.

ROSEDALE

One of the properties that the society owned was a farm that formerly belonged to Joseph Swift. A War of 1812 veteran and native of Massachusetts, Swift settled in the area in 1817. Between 1840 and 1841, he erected a Greek Revival home that he named Rosedale. Accented with Ionian columns and Egyptian Revival interior details, the home was inarguably one of the finest in the area. The beautiful home featured outbuildings, gardens, creeping myrtle and obelisk gateposts.

In 1867, the property was purchased by the Nicholas Wilber family. It's been said that the Wilbers were spiritualists and that seances were held in the house. Other stories claim that four of Wilber's grandchildren died at the house in January 1893 from diphtheria and were hastily buried on the property. In truth, they died at the home of their parents, Miller and Hattie Wilber, in Berlin Township and were buried at Maple Grove Cemetery, not far from where the angel statue once stood. There is no evidence that the Wilbers ever held seances at the house.

It should be noted that the Light of Hope Orphanage only owned the adjoining farmland and barn. Rosedale itself belonged to Fred J. Harpster, but the building sat empty and fell into disrepair.

The Deaconess Hospital

Something that's been left out of the Gore Orphanage story until now is the fact that the society also owned a hospital in Cleveland nearly ten years before the orphanage opened in Lorain County.

On October 4, 1894, the Deaconess Hospital opened at 163 Jennings Avenue. The building was converted from a three-story home owned by a woman named Overholt of Pittsburgh and was able to accommodate up to twenty-five patients. It should be noted that this institution was not affiliated with Deaconess Hospital on Pearl Road.

For nearly four months, the charitable organization operated without incident, though concerns were voiced by neighbors that the building wasn't suitable for use as a medical facility. The building had no fire escapes, and the stairs were too narrow and steep. Only one winding stairwell led to the third floor.

On the morning of February 1, 1895, everyone's worst fears were realized. At around 10:30 a.m., smoke was seen coming from the basement, and an alarm went out. The hospital was evacuated, but the flames quickly spread and soon blocked the only stairwell leading to the third floor. Before long, a crowd had gathered on the street in front of the building. They helplessly watched in horror as a Deaconess nurse appeared in the front window on the third floor. The fire was growing behind her, and escape seemed impossible. A moment later, she turned and resigned herself to the flames.

As the fire brigades arrived and gained control of the blaze, the bodies of the victims were soon discovered. Near the back stairwell on the second floor was the body of Jacob Krause, who'd recently been admitted with a skull fracture and concussion. On the third floor, firefighters discovered the remains of eight-week-old Walter Clark, whose mother had left him at the hospital a week earlier. In the front room on that same floor were the lifeless bodies of Minnie Baumer and William Allmeyer. Allmeyer had been admitted with a fractured hip and was strapped to his bed to prevent his hip from breaking again. Baumer, a nurse, was attempting to remove the straps when she was overcome by the flames. All were killed by smoke inhalation save Baumer, who died from extensive burns. In the end, it was determined that a faulty furnace was to blame.

Four months later, the Deaconess Hospital reopened in a new facility on University Avenue. The previous hospital, though greatly damaged by the fire, was rebuilt and served as a private residence for a number of years. In 1913, it was again converted into a medical facility and became Grace Hospital. On January 4 of the following year, the building was the scene of a horrific suicide, as a woman suddenly and without reason became deranged and threw herself from the third-floor balcony. It was as if she couldn't stand to be there, and the option of death seemed preferable.

Three weeks later, a fire broke out in the building. Every floor filled with smoke, but the fire itself was contained to just one room. During recent renovations, plumbers improperly ran an exhaust line so that hot cinders from the furnace emptied into a confined space, which caused the fire. There were no injuries, but the necessity of fire escapes was again realized.

Grace Hospital, originally Deaconess Hospital, on West 14th Street in Cleveland, 1930s. Note the addition of fire escapes. *Courtesy Cleveland Public Library Photograph Collection.*

The building burned again on the morning of April 21, 1963. This time, careless smoking was the culprit. Again, there were no injuries. The old hospital was then torn down and replaced by the building that now houses the Grace Center and the Cleveland Back & Pain Management Center at 2307 West 14th Street.

As far as housing a medical facility, the original building ultimately proved to be unlucky. It's possible that the hospital fire, coupled with the fire that occurred four years later in Berne, inspired the story of the orphanage fire in Lorain County.

Investigation and Other Troubles

Berghold W. Glatz was living in Lorain when his daughter Amelea contracted tuberculosis and was sent to an infectious disease hospital. Finding that he couldn't care for their children, Amelea's husband, Julius Brunk, sent their three daughters, Dorothy, Mary and Augusta, to live at the Light of Hope Orphanage. Their son, Harry, was sent to live with Glatz.

In time, Berghold Glatz sought out his granddaughters and hoped to gain custody of them. When he arrived at the orphanage in September 1909, he found them living in the most deplorable conditions imaginable. He immediately contacted attorney and Lorain County Humane Society agent Amos E. Lawrence, who brought the case before judge Edgar H. Hinman. An investigation followed that resulted in a public hearing.

Testifying in support of Glatz's claim were three young men named Tom Baker, George Lambert and Bennie Sutliffe. All had been inmates at the orphanage. Sutliffe and many others had escaped the institution and were taken in by sympathetic families in nearby Vermilion.

The men claimed that they were forced to eat calf heads, lungs, stomachs and other refuse parts. They were also made to eat a cow that dropped dead, chickens covered in sores, unhatched eggs from the incubator and food that was cooked in pots that had just been used for boiling dirty diapers. They made claims of further abuse, stating that beatings with a loaded strap were regularly administered by overseers. What's more, the children only had baths once every two to three weeks. As many as fifteen children had to share the same bathwater.

The children lived in squalor. The dormitory windows were broken, making the rooms very cold in winter. The beds were filthy and covered in lice and bedbugs, while the bedrooms were infested with rats. It was stated that Reverend Sprunger would send the children out to work at neighboring farms during harvest time. Any money they received he took from them, claiming that it would cover their living expenses. Despite having teachers, the children weren't receiving a proper education beyond the elementary level and weren't permitted to attend public school.

Reverend Sprunger took the stand, as did his wife and a former inmate who'd been an overseer. All stated that while some of these claims were true, the severity of them was greatly exaggerated.

After hearing testimony from both sides and receiving reports from investigators, Judge Hinman ruled that the conditions at the Light of Hope were unacceptable. Gantz was successful in gaining custody of his granddaughters, and Judge Hinman ordered Sprunger to improve conditions at the orphanage. Soon after, the Ohio State Board of Health sent investigators and ordered further changes. Within weeks, the place was much improved.

Though the facility had cleaned up its act, the troubles at the Light of Hope Orphanage were just beginning. On February 2, 1910, the children were enjoying an afternoon of playing outside in the snow. Two boys, thirteen-year-old Charles Lawhead and nine-year-old Paul Burger, were sledding down the steep hill that led to the road near the orphanage. Lawhead was controlling the sled but didn't notice an approaching wagon. The sled careened into the road, and Lawhead's head was crushed beneath the wheels, instantly killing him. Burger survived with severe bruises. Charles's aunt, Millie Lawhead, claimed the body and had him buried in the family plot at Woodland Union Cemetery in Van Wert County, not on the grounds of the orphanage. As far as can be researched, Charles Lawhead is the only child who died at the Light of Hope Orphanage.

A few months later, twelve-year-old Charlie Coats was adopted to Moses and Judith Richer, well-to-do farmers from Fort Wayne, Indiana. On July 14, 1910, a neighbor witnessed Moses Richer beating Charlie's head against a windowsill on the farmhouse. He roused other neighbors, who soon found Charlie lying in a field unconscious. When he was revived, he told them of how Moses Richer had beaten him with a club, mauled him and given him a dose of turpentine. Charlie Coats died soon after as a result of his injuries.

The body was examined and found to be severely mutilated by burns and covered with over five hundred wounds, three hundred of which were bites. Chunks of flesh were missing from Charlie Coats's face, arms and back, and a few of his fingers had been torn off.

When questioned, Moses Richer claimed that the boy had been fatally kicked by a cow. He eventually confessed but pleaded not guilty by reason of temporary insanity. The insanity plea didn't work. He was found guilty of murder on November 16 and sentenced to life in prison. He was spared the gallows on account of the prosecutor and judge being opposed to capital punishment.

Less than a week later, troubles continued at the site of the orphanage. At 10:45 on the morning of November 22, 1910, a fire broke out in the three-story print shop where the *Light of Hope Monthly* was printed. Fortunately, nobody was in the building at the time of the blaze, which resulted in damages in excess of $8,000. This caused a major financial loss, as the building was uninsured. It was later found that the fire had started in the engine room.

The Orphanage Meets Its End

On September 10, 1911, John Sprunger retired and signed over the title of the orphanage to the Cleveland Bible Institute Training School. Less than three weeks later, John Sprunger suffered a stroke and died. Katharina Sprunger had her husband's remains buried in the Mennonite Reformed Evangelical Cemetery in Berne, Indiana. She had their daughter Hillegonda's remains exhumed and returned to Indiana so that she could take her repose beside her father.

The Light of Hope Orphanage closed in July 1916, when it was sold to Jesse M. Elliot of Columbus, who planned to divide the land into smaller farms. The children were moved to other orphanages. Some stayed with Katharina Sprunger and returned with her to Indiana, where she died from cancer in 1934.

The Final Disposition

In the 1920s, the road that bisected the orphanage site was named Gore Orphanage Road in honor of the old institution and the Gore Tract that it borders south of State Route 303. The Joseph Swift mansion, Rosedale, was burned down by vandals on December 1, 1923, resulting in a total loss. At the time of the fire, the house had been empty for years and was heralded in newspapers as being a haunted house. This event also could have given rise

Rosedale, the Joseph Swift House, circa 1919. *Library of Congress.*

to the legend of the orphanage fire. Just beyond Rosedale, a modern home has been built. Past that, Gore Orphanage Road is closed due to the fact that the road is crumbling into the Vermilion River.

As stated in the legends mentioned at the beginning of this section, thrill-seekers go to Gore Orphanage to hear the children crying in the darkness of night. The place that most people are actually visiting is the foundation of what was once Rosedale. Nearby stands one of the old obelisks that once graced the grounds. It has been severely damaged by vandals and is barely recognizable. The other obelisks have been taken to a newer house that stands at the top of the hill, where the boys' home once stood. The site of the girls' school is now Mantle Rock Estates to the east on Portman Road.

Most of the former orphanage property was purchased by Pelham and Gertrude Blossom, who tore down the caretakers' house and built their home on nearby Sperry Road using the salvaged wood. The foundation of the former caretaker's house sits in the woods on the west side of Gore Orphanage Road immediately before the bridge over Vermilion River. Behind this sits the foundation of the old print shop. Somewhere in the area lies Hillegonda Sprunger's original headstone, which gave rise to the legend of a cemetery—containing orphans or children of the Wilber family—being located on the grounds.

BIBLIOGRAPHY

Akron Daily Argus. July 27, 1874.

Akron Daily Democrat. 1899–1901.

Baltimore Patriot. November 24, 1819.

Baltimore Sun. September 9, 1896.

Barberton (OH) Herald. August 21, 2016.

Bennison, Victor W. *The Loop Family in America*. Penobscot Press, 1994–2012.

Bierce, Lucius Verus. *Historical Reminiscences of Summit County*. Summit County, OH: T. & H.G. Canfield, 1854.

Boston Journal. April 20, 1899.

Brown, P.J. *Map of Portage County, Ohio*. Philadelphia, PA: Matthews and Taintor, 1857.

Brown, Robert C., and J.E. Norris. *History of Portage County, Ohio: Containing a History of the County, Its Townships, Towns, Villages, Schools, Churches, Industries, Etc; Portraits of Early Settlers and Prominent Men; Biographies; History of the Northwest Territory; History of Ohio; Statistical and Miscellaneous Matter*. Portage County, OH: Warner, Beers & Company, 1885.

Canton Morning News. December 4, 1906.

Canton Repository. 1843–1957.

Celina (OH) Democrat. May 9, 1913.

Chronicle-Telegram (Elyria, OH). 1909–2007.

Cincinnati Daily Enquirer. May 22, 1861.

Cincinnati Daily Gazette. July 17, 1867.

Cincinnati Magazine. November 1992.

Cincinnati Post. 1889–1909.

Cleveland Gazette. 1909–1913.

Cleveland Herald. 1840–1855.

Cleveland Leader. 1855–1903.

Cleveland Plain Dealer. 1842–1999.

Columbia (SC) Record. November 25, 1980.

Columbus (OH) Dispatch. 1930–1943.

Conneaut (OH) Reporter. November 30, 1900.

Coshocton (OH) Tribune. January 14, 1973.

Daily Express (Petersburg, VA). December 24, 1868.

Daily Forest City (Cleveland, OH). October 3, 1853.

Democratic Northwest (Napoleon, OH). October 2, 1887.

Democratic Press (Ravenna, OH). 1884–1889.

Denver (CO) Rocky Mountain News. January 16, 1890.

Ellis, Bill. *What Really Happened at Gore Orphanage?* Self-published, 1983.

Evening Independent (Massillon, OH). July 24, 1961.

Everts, L.H. *Combination Atlas of Portage County, Ohio. Compiled, Drawn and Published from Personal Examinations and Surveys.* Chicago: L.H. Everts, 1874.

Fort Wayne (IN) News. April 19, 1899.

Fremont (OH) Journal. 1864–1868.

Frey, Russell W. *The History and Legends of Rogues' Hollow.* Rittman, OH: Rittman Press, 1958.

Gard, Ronald Max, and William H. Vodrey. *The Sandy and Beaver Canal.* East Liverpool, OH: East Liverpool Historical Society, 1952.

Gateway Press (Streetsboro, OH). April 1994.

The Gazette (Medina County, OH). October 26, 2013.

Greenville (OH) Journal. September 21, 1916.

Hatcher, Harlan. *The Western Reserve: The Story of New Connecticut in Ohio.* Indianapolis, IN: The Bobbs-Merrill Company, 1949.

Howe, Henry. *Historical Collections of Ohio: In Two Volumes. An Encyclopedia of the State, Volume 1.* State of Ohio, 1907.

Jackson (OH) Standard. March 10, 1887.

Kalamazoo (MI) Gazette. April 20, 1899.

Lehman, John H. *A Standard History of Stark County, Ohio.* Stark County, OH: Lewis Publishing Company, 1916.

Lima (OH) Daily News. 1889–1890.

Logan (OH) Daily News. September 22, 1898.

Loomis, Linn. *Here and Now—Ohio's Canals: The Sandy and Beaver Canal.* Newcomerstown, OH: Linn Loomis, 1994.

Lorain (OH) Journal. June 8, 1948.

Lorain (OH) Times-Herald. December 7, 1923.

Mansfield, Ira F. *Ohio and Pennsylvania Reminiscences.* Beaver Falls, PA: Tribune Printing, 1916.

Mansfield (OH) News Journal. 1970–2014.

Marietta (OH) Daily Leader. July 15, 1896.

Marshall County Independent (Plymouth, IN). April 28, 1899.

McKee, James A. *20th Century History of Butler and Butler County, Pa., and Representative Citizens, Volume 1.* Butler County, PA: Richmond-Arnold, 1909.

Medina County (OH) Sun. August 2, 2001.

Middletown (NY) Daily Times. January 26, 1894.

Monroe, O.H. *Lorain County, Ohio: Picturesque and Industrial Features.* Lorain County, OH: 1906.

Myers, Sharon Moreland. *Classic Restaurants of Summit County.* Charleston, SC: Arcadia Publishing, 2018.

Northern Ohio Journal (Painesville, OH). March 7, 1874.

Ohio Farmer (Cleveland, OH). May 17, 1856.

Orange County Patriot (Goshen, NY). November 23, 1819.

Painesville (OH) Telegraph. 1835–1839.

Pascoe, Patty Dahm. *Erie County, Ohio, Cemetery Census Before 1909.* Erie County, OH: Erie County Cemetery Project Volunteers, Friends and Benefactors, 1989.

Perrin, William Henry. *History of Summit County: With an Outline Sketch of Ohio.* Summit County, OH: Baskin & Battey, 1881.

Perrin, William Henry, J.H. Battle, and Weston Arthur Goodspeed. *History of Medina County and Ohio.* Chicago, IL: Baskin & Battey, 1881.

Philadelphia Inquirer. July 24, 1910.

Plymouth (IN) Tribune. November 17, 1910.

Rice, Charles Elmer. *A History of the Hole Family in England and America.* Alliance, OH: R.M. Scranton Publishing Company, 1904.

Richmond (VA) Whig. December 22, 1868.

Salem (OH) Daily News. 1893–1894.

Sandusky Register. 1849–2017.

Sandusky Star. 1899–1920.

Scene Magazine (Cleveland, OH). September 30, 2015.

Stark County (OH) Democrat. March 25, 1875.

The State (Columbia, SC). August 31, 1975.

Summit County (OH) Beacon. 1881–1887.

Tiffin (OH) Weekly Tribune. June 25, 1858.

Triplett, Boone. *Canals of Ohio: A History and Tour Guide*. Wadsworth, OH: Silver Sassafras Publications, 2011.

Troutman, K. Roger. *Ohio Cemeteries: 1803–2003*. Bellville: Ohio Genealogical Society, 2003.

Trump of Fame (Warren, OH). August 23, 1871.

Tyndall, John Wilson, and Orlo Irvin Lesh. *Standard History of Adams and Wells Counties, Indiana*. Adams County, IN: Lewis Publishing, 1918.

Van Tassel, David D., and John J. Grabowski, editors. *The Encyclopedia of Cleveland History*. Bloomington: Indiana University Press (in association with Case Western Reserve University and the Western Reserve Historical Society), 1996.

Wadsworth (OH) Post. December 10, 2012.

Western Christian Advocate (Cincinnati, OH). July 25, 1849.

Wickham, Gertrude Van Rensselaer. *Memorial to the Pioneer Women of the Western Reserve*. Ashtabula County, OH: Ashtabula County Genealogical Society, 1896.

Williams Brothers. *History of Geauga and Lake Counties, Ohio*. Philadelphia, PA: Williams Brothers, 1878.

Woodyard, Chris. *Haunted Ohio*. Beavercreek, OH: Kestrel Publications, 1991.

www.bostontownship.org.

www.cleveland.com.

www.clevelandhistorical.com.

www.deadohio.com.

www.facebook.com.

www.findagrave.com.

www.ghostsofohio.org.

www.ohio.com.

www.ohioexploration.com.

www.ohioforgotten.com.

www.taverneofrichfield.com.

www.weirdus.com.

www.youtube.com.

Yesteryears (Salem, OH). July 6, 1991.

ABOUT THE AUTHOR

William G. Krejci was born in Cleveland, Ohio, in 1975 and raised in the neighboring suburb of Avon Lake. With an interest in local history, he spends much of his time debunking urban legends and works as a seasonal park ranger at Perry's Victory and International Peace Memorial at Put-in-Bay, Ohio. During the off-season, he resides in Cleveland and serves as the resident historian at the Franklin Castle. He is the author of *Buried Beneath Cleveland: Lost Cemeteries of Cuyahoga County* (The History Press, 2015) and *Haunted Put-in-Bay* (The History Press, 2017) and is the coauthor of *Haunted Franklin Castle* (The History Press, 2017). He is also the author of the Jack Sullivan Mysteries and has been a guest speaker at many local historical societies, libraries, bookstores and civic group meetings. He's appeared as a guest on the Syfy Channel's original series *Ghost Hunters* and has been featured on many local television and radio programs. He is also the cohost of the Haunted Put-in-Bay Ghost Walk with his friend Viktoriya Zakharova. In his free time, he sings and plays guitar in an Irish band.

Visit us at
www.historypress.com